The View from Here

Reflections on the Deep North, the Wild East

Franklin Burroughs

Camden, Maine

Down East Books

An imprint of The Globe Pequot Publishing Group, Inc.
64 South Main Street
Essex, CT 06426
www.GlobePequot.com

Distributed by NATIONAL BOOK NETWORK

British Library Cataloguing in Publication Information available

Library of Congress Cataloging-in-Publication Data
ISBN 978-1-68475-188-4 (hardback : alk. paper)
ISBN 978-1-68475-189-1 (electronic)

∞™ The paper used in this publication meets the minimum requirements of American National Standard for Information Sciences—Permanence of Paper for Printed Library Materials, ANSI/NISO Z39.48-1992.

Contents

Preface

In the summer of 2016, I was invited to take over *Down East* magazine's monthly column, "Room With A View." My first essay, more or less introducing myself, appeared in August of that year. My valedictory one, two years and four months later, was in the December 2018 issue. The space available for these columns was strictly limited — 650 words. Subsequently, the magazine ran a somewhat longer essay, "Up to Camp," in 2004, and a substantially longer one, "Catch and Release," in 2022. In all, my writings for the magazine amounted to about 22,000 words — enough for a pamphlet at best.

My columns, meant to be relevant to the particular month in which they appeared, were all what may be called occasional pieces. The rest of this book, the greater part of it, also consists of occasional writings — that is, writings I've been asked to contribute to an anthology, pamphlet, organizational newsletter, etc., or talks I've been asked to give. These requests provided me with a topic. They also had a word limit. It was not as miserly as the 650 word count imposed by the magazine, and was always implied rather than stated. But as a matter of common decency, if you know you are going to be sharing space with a number of other writers, you don't want to hog it. The same is true if you are giving a talk. Edward Everett, that famous and forgotten orator, spoke for more than two hours commemorating the dead at Gettysburg. Then President Lincoln read his remarks — 272 words, about one third of one "Room With a View" columns.

Lincoln, a great American writer, never wrote a literary essay. All his writings were occasional, most of them speeches. I don't know about him, but I have never found that occasional essays were easier to write, or less satisfying when completed, than any other kind of writing. In the two-volume Library of America edition of Lincoln's prose, we hear the same man, conscience, and voice on every page. I hope and believe that is also the case in this unimportant book.

— Franklin Burroughs

Room With a View
(the *Down East* magazine columns)

The first significant room with a view was a childhood bedroom. That was more than threescore years ago, on the eastern seaboard about a thousand miles south of Bowdoinham, where I now live. I was 10, going on 11. Because of some indeterminate symptoms, a fancy specialist up in Wilmington, North Carolina, condemned me to six months of bed rest, the opiate of the puny. For the first couple of weeks, I felt sick enough not to mind. Thereafter, I read, slept, looked out of the window, and wondered why he hadn't simply prescribed euthanasia.

Lying on my back, as I was supposed to do, I could only look out at the crowns of the hardwoods that had grown in along the ditch bank behind the house. A couple were dogwoods, the prettiest tree of all, but the one I remember was a wild cherry. I'd been put to bed in February, and so when March came, I could watch its slow, magical leafing out.

Like every other boy in town, I'd done my share of tree climbing and knew that its silky-green crown was unreachable for anything heavier than a squirrel. Still, I fantasized about

9

constructing myself some kind of nest and living up there, weightless, surrounded by the sun-dappled dancing of the leaves and looking down on life.

Mama brought home from the library what were deemed appropriate books for fifth graders; I read them at a clip of two or three per day. Friends of my parents dropped off books they thought I might enjoy. It says something about my boyhood tastes that one of these was a deluxe, illustrated edition of Teddy Roosevelt's *African Game Trails*, his account of a safari taken in his post-presidential years. I read it and re-read it, staring at the illustrations for so long that, for years afterwards, the sight of them gave me a feeling of convalescent lassitude.

All of this — the confinement, the view, the cherry tree, and the books — was the beginning of a lifelong love-hate relationship with claustral spaces and literature. Part of me flourishes and part of me frets in it. Reading requires enclosure and a total immersion, as sentence after sentence and page after page unfurl from their beginnings, more like music to me than music is. I can't read outdoors; I'd sooner try to watch a movie at a basketball game.

Other rooms, other views. Always, it seems, I have looked out on or into a particular tree: from different offices or classrooms, from the houses I have lived in, and from the one I live in now. There is a kind of latent animation in a tree, or perhaps, in May, a hyperkinetic one: a pair of black-throated green warblers, flitting and fluttering, the male pausing now and then to squeak out his wispy, lisping song — busy,busy,bus-SEE! Once, in an early morning class, I glanced over the heads of my drowsy but dutifully attentive students and into the upper branches of a big red oak. Not ten feet beyond the window at the back of the classroom, sprawled over a limb as though sleeping off a night of debauchery, was a massively, flagrantly inattentive raccoon.

Certain experts say our species feels happiest and most at home in situations that provide us what they call "prospect and refuge." Landscape paintings typically balance these elements — a view opening out to the horizon but containing within it places of concealment for ambush, shelter, or security. Their appeal is perhaps atavistic, a nod to our hunter-gatherer past, when such landscapes improved the odds of survival; or perhaps psychological, our minds alternately looking out at the world, then inward upon themselves. I hope these "Room with a View" essays will have something of the same effect.

SEPTEMBER 2016

On the highway between Solon and Bingham, a sign indicates you're exactly equidistant between the equator and the North Pole. On the calendar, we're approaching the autumnal equinox. The hours of daylight and of darkness are the same all over the world; all over the world, we are equidistant between the winter and summer solstices. And every year, I pass through Bingham at about this time, headed up to camp for a last couple of days of fishing.

In late September, every day is an everyday event, but also a portal, looking back into summer and forward toward winter. After the August doldrums, life quickens again: fish, birds, tourists. The north comes south: waterfowl arrive out on Merrymeeting Bay, flickers and hawks materialize out of thin air. The south comes north: leaf peepers from Massachusetts and Connecticut in big chartered buses.

At this season, anybody old enough to think of childhood as something that has gone and won't return grows susceptible to delusions of nostalgia and anticipation. Migration itself is procreative, forward-looking, but also perhaps a kind of homesickness. The bobolinks in our fields, their nesting done, yearn for the pampas of Argentina.

The fish I fish for are not exempt. Back in the prehuman past, they lived at sea and came into the rivers to spawn. Now, the lakes and reservoirs are their Atlantic; they overwinter in Wyman Reservoir, Indian Pond, or Moosehead, not somewhere off Greenland. But by September, their old impulse awakens; soon, they will be pushing up into the skinny water of tributaries, where they will prepare their redds and spawn as they did millennia ago.

Up beyond Bingham, the first leaves are beginning to turn; leaf-peeping season is just a couple of weeks away. But the fish — landlocked salmon and brook trout — have turned already, taking on their spawning colors. Male salmon darken to bronzy brown, and their lower jaws grow out. They look like a salmon becoming a pike. The females look more salmon like than ever — broader in the flanks and more silvery, more like what you find in the display cases at Shaw's or Hannaford's. The brook trout? OMG. Beautiful at any time of the year, more beautiful now: the colors more vivid, the lower flanks and belly suddenly a solid brick red.

September fishing is the Little Girl with the Little Curl. Romantically preoccupied, the fish are off their feed, sulky, finicky even by their standards. Finally, one rises — a quiet swirl over in the shadows under a ledge. You cast to it and cast again. Two or three minutes later, it rises once more, but not to your fly. By now, you are on automatic pilot, drifting exactly the same fly over exactly the same spot. The 30th cast is no different from the 31st. On the 32nd, the fish takes, is hooked, and jumps — all one action. A female salmon, brightly and broadly glittering against the sleek green water and the dark shadows behind her, sudden and startling as a Roman candle. And phht! Gone in the instant you register its arrival.

You have what you came for. Time to paddle back downriver to the truck, drive back through Bingham, return home to wait on the fine season to come, and the long one that follows.

At the North Pole, the sun now sets for half a year of darkness. At the equator, the equinox is perpetual, seven days a week, 52 weeks a year, winterspringsummerfall. What do they dream about down there?

October 2016

Vacation, vacuous, vacancy, evacuation, vacuum. The root signifies emptiness, abhorrent to nature and innkeepers alike.

So, for a vacation, in the strict sense of the word, I suggest Disneyland in Anaheim, or Disney World in Orlando, Tokyo, Shanghai, Hong Kong, or Paris. Maybe London Bridge, meticulously reassembled in Havasu City, Arizona, or Sturbridge Village or Colonial Williamsburg. These are the true vacationlands, abhorred by nature, empty of reality, unpredictability, and any human contact not involving a credit card.

I love, honor, and respect almost everything about Maine except its license plate. There is something abject about *Vacationland*, as though the state had no substance — no history, no distinct character, complexity, sophistication, cussedness, or claims of its own, as if it existed only as a sort of high-class amusement park, where people from elsewhere go when they need a break from reality. "The vacant into the vacant," to quote T.S. Eliot.

Henry David Thoreau came to Maine three times as a tourist. He traveled light, fared hard, and spent little: food for himself, his companion, and a guide consisted chiefly of pork and hardtack (dry, unleavened bread), plus fresh fish and berries, procured along the way. Gear included some rubber bags to keep their food, matches, and clothing dry; an A-frame tent, 6-by-7 feet square and 4 feet high at the ridgepole; an axe, pocketknife, and a few utensils and kettles for cooking and eating; some twine and fishhooks. Food and gear cost $24 for twelve days; the guide and canoe cost a dollar-and-a-half a day, or $19 in all. A railroad ticket for three men and a canoe from Bangor to Greenville was about $8, making a total expenditure of not quite $50, provided "you already possess or can borrow a reasonable part of the outfit."

Thoreau seems to have done no shopping while in Maine, although Bangor, that "star at the edge of night," overflowed with the refinements and luxuries of Europe and was entirely up to date. A few miles beyond, the Passamaquoddy and Penobscot tribes lived as they had for eons, which meant that all the ages of history co-existed in mid-19th-century Maine — more than sufficient reason for travelers to venture there, although none of them would have called it Vacationland, least of all Thoreau. He sought information, a wider perspective, the substrate of human existence: "rocks, trees, wind on our cheeks! The *solid* earth! the *actual* world! The *common sense! Contact! Contact! Who* are we? *Where* are we?"

Thoreau lived all of his life in Concord, Massachusetts — no writer more strictly local than he. Yet he described himself — accurately, I think — as a "soujourner": not so much a day tripper as an explorer/discoverer. A single vowel separates *vacation* from *vocation*. Wherever Thoroeau was — on the backside of "Ktaadn," along Nauset Beach, in the White Mountains, or in the hardscrabble, gone-to-seed farm country west of his house in Concord — his way of living conflated the two words and what they meant.

He is no model for everyman and had no desire to be; he was as singular as they come and wanted you and me to be that way too. We probably aren't capable of it. But his insistence that vacationland is also vocationland seems to me valuable, for both those of us who live and work in this state and those who only visit. Reality begins at home but does not end there; we travel to renew and extend our contact with it, not to escape it.

November 2016

There he is, flying in midstride. Arms raised and palms out, like a haloed saint blessing the faithful while being bodily lofted heavenward. Instead, the boy appears to be blessing the blue, wind-wrinkled water; the late-afternoon, late-summer sunlight; the deep-shaded woods on the opposite shore. His brown hair is momentarily golden; sunlight outlines his fingers, hands, arms, torso, and legs — a full body halo, a moment of grace arrested from my grandson's once-in-a-lifetime seventh year on this planet, among these seasons.

His mother, standing on the rock, above and behind him, took the photograph. From that angle, the resemblance between her son and the girl she was, thirty summers ago, is striking, and more than skin deep.

Now we are at the beginning of November. The elections are upon us. For over a year, politics have only exacerbated a ferocious tribalism, at the cost of any serious consideration of the art of the possible. Whatever their results, they will only increase our strident self-division and our implacable refusal to acknowledge facts, much less face them.

Locally, we've had a hotter and much drier summer than usual. But Maine is still Maine — those woods, that water. It's easy enough to tune out politics, even local ones, and treat the news from Washington, Aleppo, Augusta, etc., as mere rumors. Civilization has survived the insanity of world wars, genocides, and economic chaos before; somehow, we'll do it again. I want to tell myself that the scene my grandson blesses and embodies will endure.

Globally, every month of the year has exceeded its average temperature, often by a wide margin. Floods, droughts, and storms have increased in frequency and intensity. But tribal politics can always dismiss that as mere weather. We survive meteorological calamity just as we do historical calamity. That is what we tell ourselves.

We've known about rising sea levels a long time, but their consequences have been mostly elsewhere, threatening tribes on obscure Pacific atolls; Inuit villagers along the Bering Sea. Not in Maine, not so's you'd notice.

But now you'd notice. From Boston down to Miami and around to New Orleans, Galveston, and Houston. For complex reasons, the pattern of rising is uneven — faster in some places than in others, then slower, then faster again. But the trend is always upward.

If you live — as so many Americans do — within a few feet of the high-tide line on the Gulf, mid-Atlantic, or South Atlantic coasts, you don't need graphs and charts to know that seas are rising. Five or ten times last year (Boston, New York), or 40 or 60 or 80 times (Charleston, SC; Annapolis, MD; Wilmington, NC), tidal flooding closed roads and causeways for a few hours, killed the grass in yards, even came into kitchens. This is called nuisance flooding. It requires only a spring tide and an onshore breeze and can occur on a perfect summer day. In thirty years, it will no longer be flooding. Houses, neighborhoods, communities will be abandoned, despite many expensive efforts at local mitigation. By then, we may somehow have come to our senses and begun to take action, but the global tide and global temperatures will go on rising far into the future, with consequences too vast and interconnected to comprehend.

And in thirty years, my daughters may have grand-children. One day, she may even show them this essay. Our planet, our seasons, will be to them mere rumors, fables from an antidiluvian world.

DECEMBER 2016

On Christmas Day, on Christmas Day in the morning, we saw
— what? Three ships come sailing in? Mommy kissing Santa
Claus? Ten lords a-leaping? Bethlehem, deeply and dreamlessly
a-sleeping? Sleighs gliding down snow-banked roads, harness
bells a-jingle, frock-coated, hat-tipping Father at the reins,
Mother and children wrapped in furs or blankets, calling out season's greetings to friends and neighbors? An immaculate landscape, a white Christmas, a winter wonderland?

None of the above. The images of Christmas that came to
us fused and confused geographies, histories, and iconographies:
the stony, semi-arid, goat- and sheep-herding Holy Land with
its jumbled, inhospitable terrain; the deep-forested European
north, where the dire winter cold and darkness threaten to en-
gulf the world forever.

Through some combination of its religious culture, its climate, its pastoral economy, its topography, and its commercial
genius, 19th-century New England — farms and villages but-
toned up against the cold, logs blazing on the hearth, and snug
domesticity — became the American homeland of Christmas,
even in South Carolina, where I was raised. Our Christmas cards
might have been landscapes from the Holy Land or Victorian
London, but instead they mostly showed generic scenes of the
New England winter. The Christmas trees that went on sale in
my town were fir or spruce from somewhere up that way, never
one of our indigenous conifers. In many households, the local
ecology's only contribution to Christmas was unprocessed cotton

— combed out, fluffed up, piled around the base, and draped over the lower twigs of the Christmas tree to evoke snow. It fooled nobody, and nobody ever questioned its appropriateness or considered its rich historical irony.

On Christmas Day in the morning, real snow was what we most dreamed of seeing, my sister and I. We never did. It came very rarely and always later in the winter. At best, we got frost, which in that humid, swampy, alluvial country, was thick, fuzzy, and soft, and made a glittering, if ephemeral, show on the scabby, anthill-pocked lawns of the neighborhood.

My father thought some things from the world of his growing had to change and some did not. One that did not was the Christmas tree. Every December, his kinfolk in the timber business would point him to one tract or another and tell him he was welcome to cut a tree there. He chose carefully — always a longleaf pine from a pair that grew too close together, so that removing one would free the other. The limbs and twigs of longleaf curve up like candelabra, with foot-long needles at the tips instead of candles. Once cut, the tree lacks the fragrance of New England fir — it smells like pure turpentine, evoking artists' studios or disinfectants. Even when strung with lights and hung with baubles, the tree was airy, open, and skeletal, as though a modernist repudiation of the conventional Tannenbaum aesthetic.

I moved to Maine 48 years ago. It's been a quarter of a century since our family spent Christmas in South Carolina. Instead, we cut a scruffy balsam from our woodlot, drag it in, and deck it out. A wintery vigor and sharpness, tonic in their effects, comes into the house with it, and lingers a few days. Maine often seems closer to the world I grew up in than contemporary South Carolina does. But the landscape of Christmas has turned out to be the landscape of childhood. I look out at the white Christmas we often have up here, and in the mind's eye, I see sweetgums and cypresses at the edge of the swamp. They are draped with long skeins of Spanish moss, which create an effect of antiquity, melancholy, and, strangely, peace on earth.

JANUARY 2017

In college, I learned that Thales of Miletus was a pre-Socratic philosopher who considered water the primary principle of life. On that basis, I felt an affinity. More recently, I discovered he was also an astronomer who described how to use the pointer stars of the Big Dipper to locate Polaris, True North.

January, when we inaugurate our presidents, may be the finest month for star gazing. Night falls early; dawn comes late. Go out just before bedtime and again before breakfast and you'll find the darkest darkness. The stars glitter with the cold, remote precision of the sciences our species derived from them: navigation, chronology, spherical geometry, calculus, physics, cosmology, and so forth. They wheel majestically and mysteriously over us through the night. Before bedtime in early January, Orion's downward pointing belt is just above the southeast horizon; before dawn, it is setting in the southwest. But other constellations — the Big Dipper, to name one — move west to east between sunset and sunrise.

Like many of my generation who pass as well-educated women or men, I know next to nothing about the stars. I can recognize Orion, Cassiopeia, the Pleiades, and, of course, the Big Dipper, faithfully there winter and summer alike. In the fall, I'm often up early, in a little boat, motoring down a small, winding, marshy river to go duck hunting. Mostly, I navigate by the treeline and stick to the outside curves; but when the river opens into the bay, I am, to a degree, at sea, especially when a thick mist lies over the water, as is often the case. Before bedtime, the Dipper hung low above the northern horizon, its handle pointing west;

now, it stands boldly upright on the handle, looming high over-head. It gives me Approximate North (AN). I pick out some-thing bright near the opposite horizon — Jupiter, perhaps? — to give me Approximate South (AS) and a couple of other con-spicuous luminaries to fix AE and AW. If we are at half-tide or better, those coordinates will get me where I need to be by the time — an hour or so before sunrise — I need to be there.

I like — love, in fact — doing that. I can appreciate all those unknown generations who, in every corner of the globe, in a world of great depth and great darkness, observed the night sky so religiously and rigorously that Thales, 2½ millennia ago, was able to predict a solar eclipse. Seven hundred years ago — the Dark Ages to us — one of Chaucer's Canterbury pilgrims, uneducated in any bookish way, glances up, sees the shadows of the trees equal to their height, and knowing (how?) that it is April 18, exclaims that it's already 10 o'clock in the morning, and time's a'wasting. At any hour of night, any season of the year, he could have glanced at the Dipper — "Charles's Wagon" to him — and known how long 'til sunup.

But on a lower tide, when I'm trying to stay within a nar-row, sinuous channel through flats covered by a foot or less of water, my seat-of-the-pants celestial navigation doesn't work. I need, and refuse to own, a navigational system with a robotic voice saying turn left here, go 200 yards, bear right, etc., etc. I am under the stars, benighted in the shallows, churning up mud, with time and tide running out. It feels like an old man's life; it feels like contemporary history; it feels like the dark ages and the human condition. *Calm down*, I tell myself, we tell ourselves. *Consider your situation.* Consider: *con* = study; *sidera* = the stars. There's some solace in it.

FEBRUARY 2017

We began keeping chickens soon after we came to Maine about half a century ago. Over the years, we've lost a lot to predators, mostly raccoons. We never see them, only the carnage, but we see foxes in the vicinity pretty often. One trots up, usually late in the afternoon, sniffs briefly around the door and windows, then trots away, like a security guard making the rounds. These snowy mornings, we regularly find tracks from the night before. It's as if they come by as a matter of ritual rather than with any real hope — about the way some of us go to church or Fenway Park. But their tradition antedates the Red Sox and other known religions by quite a stretch.

Chickens are domesticated jungle fowl, probably from Southeast Asia. Mitochondrial DNA tells that story, back from before the dawn of civilization. Ever since, they've gone wherever we've gone. And in the Northern Hemisphere, wherever chickens arrived, foxes were waiting. Stories about the likes of Foxy-Loxy and Henny-Penny (aka Chicken Little) go back through varied cultural traditions at least 25 centuries. For most of that time, chickens and owners led beleaguered lives. Farmers, their families, and their livestock withdrew into stockaded villages or towns at night. Hens roosted under eaves, on hay mangers, or inside, with the family.

Imagine the outer darkness of those nights: moors, wastelands, forests, and fens, places no one visited. Try to imagine the inner darkness as well — ignorance, isolation, xenophobia, with hunger a constant reminder that starvation was one failed crop or sick cow away. Witches, monsters, well poisoners, marauders, ghouls, and trolls colonized the darkness beyond the walls and the psyches of the people inside them. Fear was endemic, one false alarm away from epidemic.

Only children know that kind of fear, so we tell them a version of the Chicken Little story to help free them from it. An acorn bonks you on the head, you think the sky is falling and race around telling everyone. But nothing bad happens. The world is safe — don't be such a chicken-hearted cluck. Now goodnight, sleep tight, see you in the morning bright. That was how I heard it and how I told it.

The original version was different. Foxy-Loxy throws the acorn, beans Chicken Little, then persuades her the sky is falling and destruction is at hand. Soon the hens are in an uproar.

Foxy calms them: *You know how smart I am, right?* He leads them to an underground shelter, ushers them in. There they find cubs and mother at the table, bibs tucked in, paws clutching forks and knives.

That story says that even in a dangerous world, fearmongering is a greater threat than monsters. Gullibility and the giddy, contagious thrill of scary stories create imaginary enemies and deliver us to real ones, sure as shooting.

Consider Walt Disney's 1943 cartoon version of *Chicken Little*. Thwarted by a fence around the poultry yard, Foxy-Loxy consults a psychology text and applies its maxims. First: *To influence the masses, aim for the least intelligent.* Second: *If you tell a lie, don't tell a little one. Tell a big one.* So, he persuades Chicken Little the sky is falling. The story gains traction, but is pooh-poohed by Cocky-Locky, leader of the flock. Foxy returns to his text: *Undermine the faith of the masses in their leaders.* He starts a whispering campaign — Cocky-Locky has totalitarian ambitions. It works. The final maxim, *Use flattery to make insignificant people look upon themselves as born leaders,* takes us back to Chicken Little. With Foxy-Loxy coaching her from behind the fence, Chicken Little persuades the flock to flee to a cave, escaping destruction. Sure.

All Foxy's textbook quotations are paraphrased from *Mein Kampf.* The final scene shows Foxy, belly bulging, picking his teeth with a wishbone, then sticking it into a little graveyard, where other wishbones are lined up like tombstones. The narrator protests, *Hey, that's not the way it ends in my book!*

Foxy grins and replies, *Oh yeah? Don't believe everything you read, brother.*

MARCH 2017

*"I don't know which is more discouraging,
literature or chickens." — E.B. White*

By nature or nurture, writers sometimes get broody, sit at the desk, sulk, and expect something to happen. It's the same from time to time with laying hens — *broodiness*, the instinct to incubate — hasn't been bred entirely out of them.

Reach your hand under a brooding hen. You'll get a sharp peck, and may find no eggs at all. Ask a broody writer how it's going at your own risk.

Thoreau, in his journals, wonders if brooding hens suffer from ennui, sitting in the dark corner of a barn while the rest of the flock scratch, peck, and potter around outside. He knows the feeling — he loves being outdoors above everything else, but sitting and writing are as necessary to it as exhalation to inhalation. He hasn't got much time for people. Chickens appear to be his favorite bipedal species.

A deadline looms, but a writer can have his breakfast, can't he? He has to tend to his chickens, doesn't he? He's stalling, isn't he? As he opens the henhouse door this morning, of all mornings, one of the hens bolts past him. He lunges. She panics, runs, flies, and runs some more over the yard and into the woods, squawking bloody murder.

He swears. He needs to be brooding at his desk. He fetches a poultry hook from the barn and stamps off after her. She's just inside the woods. The canny writer flanks her, gets behind her, and tries to maneuver her back toward the house. The canny hen then flanks *him* and tries to maneuver deeper into the woods. Thus, the two of them, intellectually deadlocked, make their way around the yard.

Thoreau observes that chickens, the most domestic of all domesticated livestock, allowed to range freely through the yards and streets, are nevertheless "a little shyish" around people, as though we and they were still at the very beginning of our ancient relationship. In Concord, they return every night to roost in their barn or shed and always lay their eggs there, but never become entirely trusting.

Certainly, this morning's escapee doesn't. But finally, she begins to pant: panic and exhaustion have taken their toll. Whereupon our discerning writer notices something interesting. She changes the game from tag to hide-and-seek. *And she knows exactly how to play it.* She picks a snowless spot at the base of a tree, and freezes, head down and with the tree trunk directly behind her. No part of her is silhouetted against the snow. She lacks the cryptic plumage of a grouse or woodcock, but her technique is flawless.

Philosophically, the writer considers. She, her cohorts, and their ancestors for many generations have hatched in incubators and fledged out under artificial light, with no mama hen to keep them warm and show them the ropes. Thereafter, most have lived in foot-square cages, eating, drinking, defecating, and laying eggs, until one day their lives, such as they are, get snuffed out like candles.

Not looking her way but talking to her in a conversational manner, the foxy writer repeatedly sidles toward her as she lies still and finally gets close enough to snake the hook forward beyond her leg, snatch it back, and grab her. Once tucked under his arm like a football, so she can't flap, she calms down and re-covers her matronly self-possession. Bird and man are back on good terms by the time he deposits her on the floor with the other hens.

The writer returns to his desk with something to brood about, turn over in his mind the way the brooding hen, guided only by instinct, turns over the eggs she incubates. That guaran-tees nothing, of course.

April 2017

Vacationland conjures two images — the rockbound coast and the North Woods. You pays your money and you makes your choice. As both causes and effects, *images* connect to *imaginations*.

For some, the image in the mirror is as far as reflection goes. But mostly, we crave more. Maine's coast, mountains, and big woods provide a sense of spaciousness and a possibility of adventure, thrilling to contemplate — mirrors in which we catch glimpses of unseen, unsuspected selves. The epic of American grandeur underlies them: spacious skies, purple mountain majesties. But these, and their effects on us, are not my subject, which lies instead in the unremarkable territory separating coast and North Woods: the towns, villages, small farms, and pastures.

And the woodlots: 'tis of these I sing.

Seen from the highway, as you speed toward Baxter, Sugarloaf, or Mount Desert, the little towns all look alike. You need some acquaintance with one of them to appreciate their many differences — topographic, economic, cultural, demographic, historical; their patterns of land use; the ways their pasts are hidden or revealed by their landscapes.

By American standards, they are old. The populations and prosperity of most peaked in the middle decades of the 19th century; they have exceeded it only recently, if at all. As a result, they share a common feature — what the English landscape connoisseur William Gilpin called *interrupted woodlands*: cleared land that has reverted to forest. From the outside, they appear to be immutable natural facts, like ponds or hills. But venture in and you find stone walls, scattered apple trees, borrow pits, rusted bits of barbed wire, occasional cellar holes, abandoned quarries, or old abutments. These things remind you that a century or less ago, this was an utterly different landscape — almost as bare as the Great Plains or blueberry barrens, with sweeping views from every hill or knoll. It represented a victory of human purpose over natural process, achieved family by family over years of unremitting labor. Now, natural process has reclaimed the field. Literally.

In the aggregate, such woodlands have quantifiable value, as sources of lumber, pulp, and firewood — and as carbon sinks, which mitigate the effects of atmospheric pollution. They have allowed deer, raccoons, coyotes, beavers, fishers, turkeys, pileated woodpeckers, and goshawks to recolonize much of Maine. A century ago, all were regionally rare and often locally extinct.

Another benefit is unquantifiable, but quite apparent when you walk from open land into woodland. Your way of walking — therefore of thinking — necessarily changes. You cannot stride, pace, or bustle. *Elsewhere*, the pedestrian's normal objective, is replaced by *here*; *then* by *now*. Perspectives are short and screened; they open and close ahead of you and above you as you move. There is an ambient suggestion of fluidity — the rippling patterns and patches of light and shade; the creak and flutter of trunk and leaf. You are submerged in a fresher, cooler, and airier atmosphere.

I generally go into the woods for practical purposes — to cut wood, hunt, look and listen for spring warblers, and, especially, to escape from literature. Yet the experience of being there turns out to be analogous to the best of reading, which is of course re-reading. You're not in a hurry to get to the end of the book.

Your mind is at once passively receptive and actively responsive, as though you were writing even as you read, noticing and remembering, but also generating thoughts peculiar to yourself.

These woods are full of interest, as natural history and as living monuments to economic history. They are also sanctuaries and, with minimal supervision, nurseries: children take to them the way they take to each other. It is a mistake to overlook them or to assume that, culturally speaking, their highest and best use is for housing developments.

MAY 2017

Light Hendrickson. Trout fly pattern, mimicking *Ephemerella subvaria*. Wings: flank feathers, drake wood duck. Hackle and tail: natural blue dun rooster neck. Body dubbing: urine-burned red fox.

Edward Fitzgibbon. Irish writer. Born, Limerick, Ireland, 1803. Brilliant stylist, conversationalist, and fisherman; incurable alcoholic. Squandered his gifts in gab and journalism. Wrote under the pen name *Ephemera*, certain his name and work were destined for oblivion. Died, London, 1857.

Ephemera was also another name for mayflies and is still part of the scientific moniker of many species: e.g., the above-mentioned *E. subvaria*. The strict meaning of *ephemeral* is *of one day's duration*. Most mayflies last little, if any, longer than that. Ditto most books, essays, and literary reputations — bubbles upon the stream. Poor EF!

But wait! EF wrote a book about fishing. It has hundreds of predecessors and successors in his country and ours, in his century, the next, and the one after that. His was the first to feature illustrations of prominent mayfly species, as they appear for the few seconds they sit upon the water before taking flight, juxtaposed with the trout flies (tied by EF himself) that imitate them. The book was a pioneering classic in the immense bibliography of Anglo-American dry-fly fishing. EF lives!

A.E. Hendrickson. Scarsdale, New York. CEO, swanky sportsman, and bubble upon the stream. He wrote not; neither did he tie flies. In May 1916, he fished the Junction Pool, on the Beaverkill River in upstate New York. The place is to our national history of dry-fly fishing what Independence Hall has been to our history as a democracy. Trout were feeding; a hatch of mayflies — *E. subvaria* — was underway. His guide, Roy Steelrod, examined some of the mayflies, subsequently concocted the fly described above, and two years later, knowing the side whereupon his bread was buttered, named the fly in honor of Hendrickson.

Consider: a) Wood duck were, by 1916, nearly extinct. Two years later, hunting them was outlawed. Killing or possessing one cost you $500 — that's $9,000 in today's money. The drake's flank feathers are lemony yellow, lightly barred with black. *E. subvaria*'s wings resemble wrinkled cellophane. b) Roosters with suitable hackles were rare; those with light blue-gray hackles were much rarer and priced accordingly. The legs and tail of *E. subvaria*, meanwhile, are almost transparent. c) Urine-burned fox? Geezus! Give us a break! For obvious anatomical reasons, only vixens possess the requisite pelage — a patch of fur you could cover with a postage stamp. The body of *E. subvaria*, meanwhile, ranges in color from white to tawny. You could sweep up what you needed from the floor of an animal shelter any day of the week. Is Steelrod some kind of wise guy or what?

Nevertheless, Steelrod's Hendrickson recipe passed down from generation unto generation. Furthermore, fishermen now refer to *E. subvaria* itself as the Hendrickson. The Hendrickson hatch is one of the eagerly awaited events of the trout season.

Yours truly (1942–20??). AKA *Ephemerella subliteratus*. These

x

days, wood duck are fair game and quite common. You can shoot your own or buy the flank feathers from Bean's. Genetic modification has produced roosters that provide perfect blue dun hackle feathers at affordable prices. Antron yarn — tougher than fur — is available in a color called urine-burned fox. The classic light Hendrickson pattern has been replaced by others, simpler to tie and more lifelike.

But fishing's a faith-based activity. Faith, the love child of Hope and Despair, is almost indistinguishable from her cousins, Superstition and Tradition. Fishing a fly in which you have no faith is fishless fishing. Each winter, I still tie some classic Hendricksons, cast them upon the waters in May, the most ephemeral of seasons, and consider faith, Fitzgibbon, Hendrickson, time's running stream, and whatnot, . . . and catch the occasional trout.

JUNE 2017

I've lived here fifty years. I'm deportation-proof. And loyal too — don't want to live elsewhere or otherwise. Can't imagine it, in fact.

This doesn't make me what some of my neighbors are, or what I was in Horry County, South Carolina: a native, born into a web of first cousins, first cousins once removed, second cousins, second cousins once removed, in-laws, etc. Just about everybody in Horry belonged to such a web. Because there hadn't been much in-migration, the webs connected and reconnected, generation after generation. No need for family reunions — it would have been like having a class reunion while you were still in school.

Such situations breed double-barreled homesickness — sick of home, then sick for it. Survive both and you're permanently immunized, able to contemplate your own or any other community without risking re-infection.

Since 1960, when I left for college, Horry County's population has increased five-fold, people from all over. The landscape's gone: shopping malls, golf courses, retirement communities, and amusement parks where there had been small farms, separated by patches of woods and tentacles of swamp. Driving through it nowadays is like re-reading a book whose every page has been typed over, over and over again. Gibberish.

In the past fifty years, Maine's changed too, but its landscapes remain legible, and natives still know the language: This gully you'd never thought twice about? Used to be a dam and a gristmill there. Those pilings just upstream and across from the smelt camps? They deflected the current in against the shore, where a man named Kendall had a waterwheel. It had diagonal blades, like a windmill, and a reversible gear. Three-hundred-foot driveshaft, over to Kendall's fertilizer plant, right by the railroad siding. The wheel didn't operate on dead high water or dead low — maybe a couple of hours out of the day. Otherwise, free power, 24/7, rain or shine.

Or—those old bricks in the mud, downriver from the landing? Brickworks, right there at the base of Clay Hill. Schooners could ride the tide up the Cathance, load 'em, and let the next tide take 'em back down. There's an old photograph with a two-master tied up alongside the dock.

Or—this is Ronnie, duck-guide emeritus, on the local history of a place known to every duck hunter on Merrymeeting Bay, myself included: "The Portland Gale? November, that was. She was blowing like hell up the river, and old so-and-so figured he'd walk out to the point and see was it pushing any ducks in. The point was about all pasture back then, not growed up like now. But a couple of big oaks were out toward the end, and black ducks were funneling in between 'em, just pouring into Bluff Head Cove. He stood there and shot till dark. Snow coming so heavy he couldn't hardly see — two foot or more by the time he left. Strung his ducks on a rope, dragged 'em through the snow. Fifty ducks, I heard. A hundred-and-twenty-five pounds or so."

The Portland Gale? A tragic factoid. Google it (I did): November 26–27, 1898. Hurricane-force winds. The steamship *Portland* went down, with all passengers and crew, 198 folks. Ten-foot storm surge.

Bluff Head Cove? Still there, sheltered by low-lying woods. But now, they're superimposed over an open landscape with snow-plastered, wind-whipped old so-and-so dragging his ducks across it, until at last he stands inside by the kitchen stove, snowmelt running off him like a waterfall, house creaking and groaning, he and the stove just huffing and puffing and glowing, by jeezus.

Naturalization is ongoing, and all I'll ever ask for.

JULY 2017

Every night, in the small hours, Nature calls. Sigh, slip out of the cozy bag, pad across the floor, step sockless into boots, and clump outside. Full moon, high overhead. Path to the outhouse a patchwork of moonshine and shadow; through the woods, backlighting them, the steady sheen of the lake. Having answered the call, it seems a shame to go back in, ignoring this radiant night. Why not walk down to the dock and sit a while?

Why not, but also why? To await an Epiphany? We're told they only come unbidden, to minds that lie quiet — does yours ever, ever? To be "At One with Nature?" Heaven forbid. That comes soon enough, when she calls us home, or to oblivion, or to what a metrophobic old man, much admired by Thoreau, once referred to as "Another Boston."

Nevertheless, go down to the dock, sit still, try to stifle the mental chatter. No clouds, no stars — Luna rules the night, all the earth keeping silence beneath. Light without heat, brightness without glare, an antiseptic fluorescent glow from lake and sky, but, coming across the water from the moon, a glittering beam singles you out, puts you on stage, self-conscious and limelit in an empty theater.

Well, yes. Meanwhile, a seeping, somewhat metaphysical chill reaches your bones. The sleeping bag beckons; common sense seconds. But don't we wait all year for one moment — an inhabited snapshot — to distill and arrest the quicksilver apogee of the Maine summer? Might this moony night be it? Sit and shiver some more; find yourself drifting toward unconsciousness, the outer suburbs of Another Boston.

Then, abrupt, Nature calls again: a loon, just across the cove. Not the famous lunatic laughter, but that long-held, quavering, harmonic wail that carries and carries and is reserved for mated pairs. Ornithologists tell us this is what it means:

He: *I'm over here.*

She (offstage): *Me, I'm over here.*

Their week-old chick, a blob of black fluff the size of a beanbag, may chime in with a respectable version: *I'm here too.*

No call in nature so hauntingly transcends its purpose. The sound is full of eerie seeking, as of a lost soul for a lost world. Even on a small pond, it creates auditory illusions of desolate, oceanic spaces, a call coming down from the stars or aimed at them: the most aching inarticulacy you'll ever hear in Maine, or anywhere.

Shut up; LISTEN! The male follows his *Ah WOOOoooo* with a second, more distant seeming version, like an echo. The female responds in the same fashion — two real loons crying out, then their ghostly doppelgangers.

You are hopeless. Give it up. Clomp back to camp, step out of the boots, snuggle into the bag. Nature's calls are robo-calls; we — old men, baby loons, whatever — are answering machines. We may be conscious of nature, love or fear her; she's unconscious, uncaring, unrequiting. Her commands are *Eat, propagate, die. Along the way, mate, feed and defend the young, fight or flee as per the situation. Obey thy bowels and thy bladder, by day and by night. Get some sleep.*

Unrequited consciousness, unrequited love, chronic loneliness, and angst give us only songs, poems, ads, art, adolescence, credulity, humanity, delusions of omnipotence, transcendence, lucidity — all "that hunger of imagination which preys incessantly upon life," as another dead old guy put it. Strange how loons, about the most ancient, unevolved birds on earth, stir that stuff inside us.

Summers slide away. We are *here* (for now). That's enough. That's not enough.

August 2017

Twelve centuries ago, if Old English poets (*scops*) are to be believed, the wolf *(wulf)* watched the eagle (*earn*), the eagle watched the raven (*hrafen*), and the raven watched a Viking longboat run ashore and disgorge a troop of armed marauders (*wicinga*, aka *waelwulfas* — slaughter wolves). The Vikings headed inland, with a growing entourage of wolves, eagles, and ravens. Sooner or later, they encountered the local Homeland Security detail, men similar to themselves in armor, weaponry, and bloodlust. The battle lines formed and converged. The wolves, pinch-bellied but patient, settled on their haunches and watched with intense interest. The ravens — dozens? hundreds? — circled overhead, croaking. High above them, the eagles soared.

This assembling of the Beasts of Battle is as regular a preliminary to combat in Old English poetry as the singing of "The Star-Spangled Banner" at a baseball game. These battles were sudden-death competitions. To the victors went the spoils; to the losers came those grim omens — wolf, eagle, raven — to feast and squabble.

At the mouth of the river, their counterparts are seals, ospreys, and terns. At this season, they are always there: a few terns, flickering along low over the water; an osprey or two, lumbering along or soaring, at intervals folding up and plunging; the heads of seals pocking the surface of the river from one side to the other, just lying there, facing into the current, occasionally slipping with a liquid motion below the surface. Something may happen.

A friend, repairing the deck of a nearby house for its absentee owner, heard wings, glanced up: an osprey flying over, lugging a small striper. He could no more ignore the osprey than the wolf the eagle, the eagle the raven, or the raven the longboat. He looked riverward: terns whirling close inshore; seven ospreys circling, plunging, coming up empty or coming up slow, shuddering themselves dry, and laboring off, talons locked into a small striper. All of this was happening in a succession of temporary whirls, crosscurrents, and rips the tide created close against the shore.

Three days later, just before the tide was right, he returned in full battle-rattle: chest waders, flyrod, rain-jacket, wool socks, long johns. For a while, nothing: The tide slipped by. No terns or ospreys in evidence. A few seals loafing around, some in the river, some hauled out on a mid-river ledge. Then everything began: boiling eddies formed, terns materialized, yelping and diving, then ospreys. He was waist deep in the river, catching fish, before he saw the first dark shape glide by, then another. Seals.

"I could have touched some of them with the tip of the rod," he said. "A cormorant joined them. It looked like a skinny little seal. Swam the same way too. I got maybe thirty fish in an hour. None big, but it was *neat*." He laughed. "Kind of spooky too. A couple of those seals were bigger than I am."

He invited me to join him the following morning. It dawned overcast, spitting a little rain. Seals everywhere, upriver and down. Terns too. One osprey. The tide ran out; as though by catalytic reaction, the eddies formed. Two seals swam in, heads up, hopeful as Labrador retrievers at suppertime. We cast and we cast. Next time I looked, the seals were gone. Waders, sweaters, windbreakers and all, it was hypothermically cold.

Nary a flurry of feeding, nary a fish — just all that life and death out in that river, all that expectancy in the air. The catching of fish is not the most important thing in the world. While it lasts, the fishing is — a window into the world that may open for a moment, grant you a glimpse.

SEPTEMBER 2017

Just inside the woods behind our kitchen, a feldspar outcropping was blasted about a century ago, leaving a vertical ledge that looks like an ancient ruin. Ashes and maples have grown up in the rubble at its base; ferns and moss have colonized all but the steepest parts of it. For at least 50 years, porcupines have occupied one of its deeper crannies. They are model tenants. They mind their business; we mind ours. When we happen upon one, it seems abashed and bustles off as best it can.

Early one morning this spring, I glanced out the kitchen window and found we had new tenants. A red fox cub sat on a flat rock under the bird feeder, about 30 feet away, staring intently in at me. I watched it until the coffee was ready. When I looked out after breakfast, it was curled up on the rock and fast asleep. It was about the size of a six-week-old kitten, and just as fluffy.

It turned out to have two equally un-shy siblings; the parents were more circumspect. The vixen was much the smaller — subtract the tail and she was scarcely bigger than a housecat, perhaps half the size of her mate. She would hang back in the woods while the kits came out to sun, sleep, or frolic under the bird feeder. Within two weeks, both parents spent their days hunting, leaving the kits unsupervised. The kits began venturing farther from the den, sometimes together and sometimes separately.

Red foxes are astonishingly adaptable, inhabiting most of the Northern Hemisphere, from above the Arctic Circle down deep into the tropics — deserts, alpine meadows, tropical rain-forests, the Mongolian steppes, and the Siberian taiga. But they are partial to our species and have hung around us so persistently as to inhabit a particular cranny of our collective imaginations, as evidenced by folklore, proverbs, and fables that go back for millennia, and, more recently, by nursery rhymes, children's books, and animated cartoons. They are never entirely wild and fearsome, but familiar and local, skulking around barnyards, henhouses, and rabbit hutches like pickpockets and shysters around country fairs and racetracks. In most stories, they outwit everybody, and then themselves. We apparently have a sneaking fondness for such sneaky fellows, and our stories generally let them off with nothing worse than a comeuppance and a bruise or two. They will be back; the game will go on.

As they grew accustomed to us, the kits would sit and watch, cocking their ears quizzically when spoken to, or else prancing flirtatiously. In my experience, this endearing behavior is typical, as though kits cannot decide whether people represent threats or potential playmates. Even adult foxes, at a safe distance, sit and study us attentively: they the ornithologists and we the birds. Their behavior most closely resembles that of feral cats — too familiar with us greatly to fear us; too independent to crave closer contact.

Before myth became history, did foxes — like dogs, cats, chickens, and livestock — consider the trade-offs involved and cast their fate with ours, then think better of it after a few eons? Throughout the historical past we have trapped, hunted, hounded, and poisoned them to the best of our ability. Samson caught them by the hundreds, set their tails on fire, and became a hero of the highest order. Yet they don't dread us and can't quite leave us. Behind their predatory opportunism and our persecution there seems to be a sort of reproachful longing for a might- have-been that neither species can quite ignore.

It's been a nice summer around here.

OCTOBER 2017

From the neck down, guinea fowl are handsome. European chefs rightly prize them — easily the best poultry I've ever tasted. But I can as readily imagine a lemming ranch as a commercial, EU-regulated guinea farm.

In South Carolina, tobacco allotments were small and about the only source of money. Farm families lived close to the bone. But many kept guineas, which they neither ate nor fed. The guineas cried *puhTRAK! puhTRAK!* whenever a car drove by, a hawk flew over, a door slammed, or somebody sneezed, but they also ate tobacco hornworms, which otherwise ate the precious tobacco seedlings. They roosted in trees and were regularly picked off by owls, but a few generally survived long enough to raise a brood and keep the flock going.

For reasons reason cannot elucidate, some people in Bowdoinham keep guineas. They don't eat them, can't domesticate them, and have to feed and shelter them through the winter. They hope to wake up one morning and discover the whole flock has run away and joined the circus. Instead, they remain, repeating their grating, compulsive note — *puhTRAK! puhTRAK!* from dawn to dark.

We have a neighbor who is no longer young. Call him McDonald. And old McDonald had some guineas: *puhTRAK!* here, *puhTRAK!* there; here, there, everywhere *puhTRAK!*, etc. We'd hear them in the woods behind the house or see them standing in the middle of Route 24, *puhTRAK*ing urgently. (Another, more distant neighbor also had a flock and had a customized highway caution sign — *Guinea Xing* — beside the road in front of his house. The trouble is guineas don't *X*; they *confer*, blocking traffic in both directions.)

Of course, McDonald's flock shrank, depleted by traffic, fierce wild beasts, and Hereditary Pretraumatic Stress Disorder. Finally, there were three, then two. Then there was one, a hen. McDonald named her PuhTRAK, so she could talk to herself.

One October morning, I was backing the boat into the garage — a tricky maneuver. Suddenly, there in my rearview mirror, next to the trailer's right wheel — more precisely, the right hubcap — was PuhTRAK, insistently introducing herself to her reflection. I backed the trailer against the garage's side door, opened it behind her, herded her inside, caught her, and drove her over to McDonald's. My story didn't surprise him. It turns out PuhTRAK spent most nights under his truck and a good part of every day *puhTRAK*ing away at its hubcaps. Guineas are, he explained, pathologically gregarious: *A flock's a sort of phobic reinforcement support group, I guess* — McDonald is an observant, original man — *just what we need these days*.

We saw her once more. In November, a gang of wild turkeys regularly rummaged under our birdfeeder, and one day, rummaging with them, was PuhTRAK. When they took alarm and scuttled off, she did too. We hoped she might find acceptance, a new identity, and a new vocabulary for herself.

But we heard she returned home and resumed sleeping under the truck and conversing with the hubcaps. That winter, snowbanks reduced McDonald's road to one lane. One bitter day, the sander came rumbling up it. PuhTRAK — guard dog? Miss Lonelyhearts? lunatic? — ran after it, yelping. It stopped to turn around in the last driveway. Perhaps she scrambled up the snowbank to get away, then tried to fly over the truck. Somehow, she wound up in the back of it. She was reportedly last seen in Topsham, swaying precariously atop a pile of shifting sand, southbound.

To some, her spectacular exit suggested apotheosis. Local mythographers accordingly prophesy she will one day return in glory, cry out from a high place, and our lonely nation will respond in ecstasy: *PuhTRAK! PuhTRAK!*

November 2017

Late this summer, satellite photography showed Harvey and Irma approaching. From above, they resembled cinnamon buns that had finished rising — puffy, white, and curling inward toward their centers, which looked like navels. They differed in that cinnamon buns curl clockwise and hurricanes counterclockwise, and in that the perimeter of the hurricane is ragged. Video shots showed the other difference: the fearsome energy of the hurricane, spinning off streamers of cloud and vapor like wind-tattered flames.

At the center, the lower barometric pressure pulls air inward, creating a vortex: Imagine a stovepipe inhaling, with its walls made of solid wind. Or, for another kind of analogy, think of the dark episodes of national histories. "Of silver and gold they have made them idols . . . they have sowed the wind, and they shall reap the whirlwind," as the Lord said unto Hosea. Whirlwinds are fueled by hot air, we might add.

But how sweet and mild are the lesser whirlwinds of the warm months. Once, on Attean Pond in May, three of us saw a little disturbance on the smooth water, like a school of minnows. Then it seemed to organize itself, like water circling down a drain. Vapor began to thicken and twist above it: a micro-waterspout, not much taller or wider than I am. It wavered along for ten or fifteen yards and disappeared, not a hundred feet from our canoe. No voice spoke to us out of the whirlwind, as it once did to Job, although we half expected it to.

That was once in a lifetime. More common are the dust devils of midsummer, when it's dry and dusty. One might come reeling down a country road toward you, something between a midday ghost and a gyroscope. It pulls up dust the way a tornado pulls up debris, whirling it inward instead of blowing it outward. They were fairly common in South Carolina; less so here.

A bit later, with luck, you may see on some perfectly still, weatherless day the tedded hay lift off a field and move along over it in a loose, leisurely spiral, caught in a local updraft. It goes along a few hundred yards before it dissipates, and the hay drifts back down to earth. Or to water. Once, again in a canoe, I was surprised by wisps of hay falling gently down around me. That was as close as I have come to being honored by a ticker-tape parade down Broadway's Canyon of Heroes.

The most reliable slow-motion cyclonic events of the summer are the updrafts called thermals. Migrating hawks find and define them for us. Between mid-August and mid- September, you see them kettling: some low enough to catch your eye, some so high they are little more than dust motes, even through binoculars. If the updraft rotates counterclockwise, they soar clockwise, for the same reason airplanes take off into the wind, to maximize lift. They ride to the top, then slant off southwestward. Many of them thermal-hop their way down to Central America and beyond.

In early November, if you face the sun and look upward, you may see gossamer drifting across the sky — single strands of silk, extruded from spiders too small to see. Their law is *disperse or die. Or both.* Gossamer has been found on weather balloons three miles above the earth; sailors in mid-ocean occasionally find the decks littered with it.

Gossamer comes from *goose summer*, which once meant in

England about what *Indian Summer* means to us. It passes; the spinning Earth tilts away from the sun; and on still, frigid days, smoke spirals up from our chimneys, as goose summer gives up the ghost.

FEBRUARY 2018

We moved to Maine fifty years ago and bought "a certain lot or parcel of land, with the buildings thereon," which would thenceforth be ours, then pass to our "heirs and assigns and the survivor of them, and their heirs and assigns of the survivor of them, forever." Were we buying a house or founding a dynasty that would last until the stream of time ran dry?

We've bought and sold several lots and parcels of land since then. Subtract all the lawyerly rigmarole and face it: The house you sit in and the ground you stand on are liquid assets. We hold a lease on life itself and on every other thing we think we own. Appraisers appraise, adjusters adjust, markets set prices, cash flows in and out, which is why it's called *currency*. If that current ceases, the lights go out. If you cease, it glides smoothly on, utterly unaffected.

Fifty years is a lot of water over the dam or through the turbines: the flow of time converted into productive energy or simply rolling, unmetered, toward oblivion. But after fifty years, it's time to look back and consider the water that did not go over the dam but has accumulated behind it. It will not endure until the stream runs dry, but while you last, it's there, a private reservoir.

When we were young, we meant to travel light, subconsciously assuming that would keep us from getting old. That first lot or parcel of land changed us. It was as though the deed conveyed an aspiration as well as a property: to locate ourselves in time and space, to have children who would have children; to build a private archive, a private history, and begin to become in-vested in the turning of the seasons, the passage of the years, the school board, and the conservation commission, the little news-or-gossip—worthy events that punctuated the recurrent ones.

It is February now, halfway between the winter solstice and the spring equinox, no light visible at either end of the tunnel. Maybe it's a good time to undertake some off-again, on-again program of semi-centennial reflections, to yield to the tempta-tions of retrospection. When you get old, you do that; the view behind you is so much more extensive than the one ahead.

In the past decade, I've found myself reconnecting with friends from my pre-Maine years. We belong to our generation. We belonged to a town or a graduating class at a small, rather homogenous college, or both; we speak the same language be-cause of that. And now we find ourselves far apart — geograph-ically, in the experiences that we have had, in the people we have turned into. How much of that could have been foreseen, even all those years ago? How much of it would have been different if I, for example, had returned to my hometown, as several of my friends did to theirs, or if they had spent the past fifty years in Maine?

It hasn't been hard for us to fall back into our old bantering, teasing, trusting ways. That is balanced by astonishment at find-ing ourselves so old and so incomplete, and so changed from what we once believed ourselves to be, and so unchanged. In doing this, I can hardly explain myself, or say who it is I think I have become, without reflecting on where I have lived for the past fifty years. Insofar as those reflections are about me, they are of little interest or utility to you; insofar as they are about Maine, I hope they may be.

March 2018

Fifty years ago, we moved to Maine and bought our first home, an old and modest Cape Cod cottage — four small rooms downstairs, two smaller ones upstairs, under the rafters. A towering elm stood in the side yard, ridiculously out of scale with everything around it. The tree was much younger than the house. It was quite possibly planted in 1876. That would be consistent with its size, and that was America's triumphantly celebrated Centennial Year, which also happened to be the year a winter storm blew down the famous Great Elm on the Boston Common. The coincidence occasioned a spate of patriotic elm planting throughout the country, and especially in New England.

As we settled in, Dutch Elm disease was killing off the last of the big local elms. Ours, still outwardly healthy, was doomed. You saw dead ones standing everywhere — in farmyards, front yards, along city streets. Most of them were roughly the same size as ours and appeared to have been planted at about the same time, in a nation that had survived a savage Civil War and grown from thirteen quarrelsome colonies into a continental empire over the course of a single century.

By 1968, our nation was again on the brink of disintegration, as though the dying elms portended the end of the American Experiment. But from the get-go, the prospect of imminent death has been what we signed on for. "Democracy never lasts long. It soon wastes, exhausts, and murders itself." — John Adams, 1814.

As the elms were disappearing and we were learning to live in Maine and an unwinnable war was raging in Vietnam, the Black Panthers coined their "power to the people" slogan, which was immediately appropriated by the anti-war movement. The idea behind the slogan has been deployed throughout our history. These days, neo-populists claim it, and with it, the mantle of the American Revolution: The Tea Party, the Liberty Caucus, the many self-styled militias in the mountain West. Whoever claims that legacy implicitly threatens violence against perceived Enemies of The People: "The tree of liberty must be refreshed from time to time with the blood of tyrants and patriots. It is its natural manure." — Thomas Jefferson, 1787

Back when all this got started, the Boston Common boasted another elm. It had been planted in 1646, which made it younger than the Great Elm, and it would die sooner. By 1766, John Adams, describing a meeting with other patriotic opponents of the Stamp Act, could refer familiarly to it as the Liberty Tree. Not long after that meeting, self-styled patriots hung effigies of Stamp Act proponents from its branches. Liberty trees were soon designated in other colonies. In Charleston, South Carolina, it was a majestic live oak.

During the war, Royalist forces chopped down the Liberty Trees in both Boston and Charleston, as though to destroy the rebellion at the root. Thereafter, New England's elms, long cherished as ornaments, became symbols, providing not simply shade and a certain elegance to raw, unprepossessing little towns and ordinary farmhouses, but also asserting, in the quiet, persistent way of trees, the steadfastness and growth of a country and an idea.

I assume whoever planted the one in our side yard meant to celebrate patriotic and democratic notions. But I expect he also imagined the sapling growing and in time becoming the tallest tree around — a local landmark, evidence of the prosperity, pre-eminence, and rootedness of his descendants: that is, of their status as democratic aristocrats. "Democratic aristocrat" is, of course, an oxymoron, expressing another internal contradiction that has always been with us. Jefferson was one; Adams was the mirror image: an aristocratic democrat.

Even before we moved here, the effort to locate and prop-agate disease-resistant elms had gotten underway, and it contin-ues. Thus far, this experimental undertaking cannot be said to have succeeded. Or failed.

APRIL 2018

Some random geezer stops and peers into your face. You peer back. Something familiar about him. Are you? Frank? Mark? Yes, you both see it now — you resemble your former selves as prunes resemble plums. You shake hands, happily call back friends and events from — thirty years ago? More like forty. Dear God — seems like yesterday: everything sharply detailed and in focus, more vivid now in memory than it was then in fact.

On the day they married, my parents' neighbors wedged a brick into the angle formed by the trunk and limb of a churchyard oak. They soon moved off into their lives, checking the tree on their visits home. No parishioner ever saw it grow, but it did. And as it did, the trunk and the limb slowly enveloped the brick. The last time our neighbors — Bev and Willard, dead these many years — stopped by their tree, they were nearly as old as I am now. The brick was invisible, not even leaving a bulge in the trunk.

Willard was a quiet, intense man who loved sitting alone, with the shades drawn, listening to Mozart. At those times, Bev walked over for a cup of coffee with Mama. She would already be talking as she came in the kitchen door: her natural habitat was mid-sentence. Mama, no slouch herself, said little old Bev was the talkingest woman on earth, bless her heart. What had become of the young love that wedged the brick into the tree? "About what became of the brick," I imagine my father saying.

After Daddy retired, my parents spent their summers in Maine. He and I would go up north whenever we could, to fish. We fished the river in the mornings, until an upstream dam opened, flooding out the rest of the day. Along the way to one pool, we would crunch across a gravel bar as we headed upstream early in the morning, then skirt around it on the way back, when the gravel bar had become a sloshing, foam-churned eddy.

At the upper edge of the gravel bar, a spruce, no taller than a seedling, although thicker, grew in the gravel just at the cusp of the woods. We wondered about it — in that soilless medium, how had a seed ever germinated, a seedling taken root? And how did it survive the daily inundation, which submerged it completely?

We walked that way five or six times a summer for twenty years, until Daddy was too old for it. Each year, the spruce was still there — more than knee high eventually, very dense, perfectly conical, its trunk as thick as your thumb. He frequently commented on it: "tough little joker," or "bet you'd need a microscope to count the growth rings." Something like that.

Now, 25 years later, I still walk that way every summer. Same gravel bar, same daily inundation. But there must have been a micro-eddy created by the stem of the little spruce, causing fine silt to settle out from it, because the spruce soon stood in shallow soil of its own making and began growing in earnest. A second spruce soon rooted itself behind it, then a third, then a dozen or so, making more and more soil. The forest was colonizing the gravel bar. Last year, the tallest spruce — not the original pioneer, but one farther out from the woods — was seven feet high. You wouldn't need a microscope to count the growth rings.

There are costs to being human. I've borne less than my fair share so far. When the past surfaces — a chance encounter, a long-dormant memory — it is generally benign, a happy occasion. Nevertheless, I am, let's face it, a random geezer. For decades now, I have fund a kind of happiness in noticing trees and thinking about them. It isn't rational. Happiness, alas, seldom is.

MAY 2018

I'd rather be Up North.
— bumper sticker, indigenous to Maine, typically
encountered on thoroughly used pickup trucks

Up North, in the true canoe country, early May is to canoe tripping what Thanksgiving-to-Christmas is to retailing. The whole
year quickens toward those two weeks. By Mother's Day, black-
flies are out in force, some of the best fishing of the year begins,
and one grows distracted.

Up North, early May may mimic mid-March — raw,
windy, spitting a little snow. Once I watched two good canoeists,
one of them my daughter, paddle out of the lee of Attean Mountain and turn into the teeth of the wind. She, in the stern, and
her partner, in the bow, were kneeling, leaning into every stroke
and paddling in sync, the bow never wavering to one side or the
other, the canoe steady as a weathervane. Textbook. I looked past
them to the opposite shore, to gauge their progress. They were
not progressing; the opposite shore, however, was. Perfectly
under control, making every stroke count, they were going backward. Liz gave it up, angled the bow slightly off the wind, and
kept paddling ahead, letting the wind deflect them gradually
sideways, back under Attean Mountain.

Two hours later, with Holeb Pond and its outlet stream
behind us, the sun was out, the wind somewhere up in the treetops, and we were sitting back, letting the current do most of
the work, breathing easy and making time down the Moose

River. It's narrow and convoluted there, winding among alders, its water sleek, alive, a pure and shining black, with no trace of dust or pollen on it, and that is also early May, Up North.

On that trip, maybe 25 years ago, my daughter was almost the same age I'd been the first time I paddled the Moose River Bow trip. Do the math — it tells me my days of canoe-tripping are probably behind me. *Probably*, I said.

I won't list the other trips on other rivers and across other lakes Up North, early in May. At night, when I can't sleep for some reason — having this damned essay to write, for example — I try recalling them to sedate myself. When they finally begin blurring into each other, the Seboeis no longer distinct from the St. John's from the Machias, with its red pines and blueberry barrens, it means I am about to slip under.

Were there adventures? Once, with the canoe on my shoulders, so all I could see was its inverted interior in front of me and the mucky portage trail under my feet, I nearly ran into a moose. I heard a snort, lifted the canoe bow to look, and we shared a long, aghast instant of reciprocal, interspecific incredulity. Then he turned and went off at that fast, mincing trot into the woods.

But mostly canoe tripping Up North in the prime time of early May is not about this or that thing that happened or what you chanced to see. It is not even about the pleasing constants of all such trips — setting up camp, the campfire, the tents with pine needles pattering down on them through the night, or even the familiar, fluid rhythm of paddling.

Canoe tripping in Up North in early May is about some quality of the air, something you can actually smell — slightly pungent, with hints of bay leaf, subtle retsina overtones, and the effervescence of chilled champagne, giving an overall effect of pure oxygen, deeply inhaled. This elixir cannot be packaged, bottled, or sold online. Legend says Ponce de León ransacked Florida searching for it; American consumers spend billions annually on drugs, doctors, gym memberships, and holistic horse-fodder hoping to find it. It is unattainable, but Up North, in early May, it exists. Not for long, but for real.

JUNE 2018

By 1900, the following animals were extinct or nearly extinct in Maine and everywhere else east of the Mississippi: 1) any wild canid larger than a fox, 2) wild turkeys, 3) beavers.

We got here in 1968. A few wild canids larger than foxes had recently been shot or trapped up along the Canadian border, causing high excitement. You'd have thought they were were-wolves or the Viet Cong.

A decade later, the Department of Inland Fisheries and Wildlife transplanted 41 wild turkeys from Vermont into York County, down near the New Hampshire line. They did well enough for 33 of them to be trapped and transplanted into Waldo County four years later. There had not been wild turkeys in the state since about 1800. They might as well have been ptero-dactyls; insofar as local memory was concerned. Other states were undertaking similarly modest efforts.

Beavers were doing better than turkeys, but even so, most were in northern Maine. It would be several years before I actu-ally saw one in the mid-coast area. In the rest of the country, few, if any, had spread beyond the northernmost tier of states to re-populate their historical range.

Whitetail deer were doing better still. But their North American population, estimated to have been about 35 million when the Europeans arrived and down to about 300,000 by 1900, was still far, far below historic levels.

Today, from Maine to Florida and from the Atlantic to the Mississippi, large wild canids (Eastern coyotes fortified with a bit of gray wolf DNA), wild turkeys, beavers, and whitetail deer are everywhere. Furthermore, they do not behave in the least like timid and traumatized refugees from oblivion. They act like they own the place — as though suburbs, city parks, vacant lots, golf courses, cornfields, flower beds, your hen house, and every wretched little stream or culvert across the length and breadth of this great and fruitful nation were their New Frontier, their Manifest Destiny, their City on a Hill.

In less than a century, the whitetail deer population has returned to approximately what it was when the first Europeans arrived; their range now greatly exceeds what it was then. Turkeys and beavers have come back from the dead; coywolves, or whatever we want to call them, clearly descend from the creature that has haunted the imaginations of townspeople and farmers and herdsmen and especially children more or less forever and that barely hangs on in the remotest parts of Eurasia — yet here one stands, atop some dumpster at the edge of some town, looking contemptuously down at you as though to say *What's your problem? It's a free country, right?*

Think of western Europe. Its wilderness disappeared long before ours. There may be a few enclaves where some of its once-impressive fauna — wolves, bears, beavers, the capercaillie, the Eurasian elk — survive as something more than game animals provided habitat and supplementary feed so they may be shot. But such enclaves are very scattered and very small. What has happened in the U.S. in the last half century is not at all like that. In the most densely populated, longest settled sections of the country, we have exploding populations of animals that had been gone from them for time out of mind — in many places, since before the American Revolution.

By 1968, it had become clear that Future Shock — too much change too fast — was the human condition and would remain so. The past no longer provided any guidance. I have foreseen nothing of what has happened in the past fifty years; neither has anybody else. I certainly cannot say that the return of dispossessed mammals to their ancient haunts is the most important thing that has happened in my lifetime. But it does seem to me the unlikeliest, the most paradoxical, and the most pleasing.

JULY 2018

I brought Roger Tory Peterson's *Field Guide to the Birds* with me when we moved to Maine in 1968. Its preface includes his life list of all the species he had seen in the U.S. east of the Rockies. From boyhood forward, whenever I have seen a new bird, I have checked it off his list, which runs to 426 species in all. So far, I've seen 276 of them — not quite two-thirds. With one exception, each new species has arrived serendipitously, like the red-throated loon that suddenly popped up beside my canoe on Broad Cove, in Bremen, forty years ago.

I have a distinct range and distinct habitat preferences within it. I make brief annual migrations to South Carolina, usually in April. From May to October, I range northward as far as Jackman. In the past decade, South Carolina has yielded the swallow-tailed kite, the hooded warbler, the red knot, the roseate spoonbill, and the whooping crane (the one species I didn't encounter by chance; a wildlife biologist took me to see it). Over the same decade, northern Maine has contributed the Nashville warbler, American pipit, rusty blackbird, northern water thrush, spruce grouse, and black-backed woodpecker.

On long drives, I count the species I see along the way. When my eagle-eyed granddaughter Ana is along, we make a game of it. The inevitable crows, ring-billed gulls, and grackles are worth a point (1); blue jays, red-winged blackbirds, mourning doves, and robins (2); red-tailed hawks, tree swallows, eastern kingbirds, and bluebirds (3); ospreys, wild turkeys, great blue herons, and kestrels (4); ruffed grouse (6); catch of the day (8–20

— birds in this category aren't necessarily rare, but are unlikely to be seen along a road: thus a green heron or sharp-shinned hawk rates an 8, a Cooper's hawk or merlin a 10; an American bittern or goshawk a 15, and so on).

My Peterson is the third edition, published in 1947. It's dated — asserting, for example, that cardinals, mockingbirds, tufted titmice, turkey vultures, snowy egrets, and even the common grackle do not range farther north than Connecticut. I distinctly remember the first cardinal (3), mockingbird (5), titmouse (3), turkey vulture (3), and snowy egret (8) I saw here, and how much each one pleased me — old friends from home. The snowy egrets remain somewhat uncommon, concentrated in tide flats and marshes near the coast; the others are now everywhere. Within the past five years, I've occasionally seen all of them as far up as Jackman.

But oh, Ana, the lengthening list of now-rare birds common in Peterson's time and that your mother and I still took for granted when she was your age! Meadowlarks, for example, or towhees or cliff swallows or nighthawks or whip-poor-wills, their jarring calls audible even inside the car. I last heard one 21 years ago, in a riverside thicket halfway between Solon and North Anson. Nighthawks? We called them bull-bats in South Carolina, and spoke of bull-bat hour the way they speak of happy hour up here. Three decades have passed since one exploded beneath my feet, going into her crippled-wing routine to draw me away from her nest, a little scrape in the dirt. I fear you may never see that.

Rare birds, high-value birds, please us. But no more than the cliff swallows that once arrived in abundance every spring, hovering, fluttering, and squeaking — a noise like wet leather — under the eaves of the barn, building their little gourd-shaped nests of mud pellets, or congregating around puddles, to pick up more mud, or, later on, popping in and out of the nests, abundant, squabbling, communal, and busy — part of our household for a few months. The occasional pairs I see these days are somehow forlorn, diminished. Ordinariness, Ana, makes things special. That is about the only lesson someone my age can teach someone your age. And I strongly suspect you know it already.

August 2018

A mulch of dead leaves, twigs, lichen, all browns and grays. One smooth, moist stone. "Two feet in front of the little ash," John Cullen said. "Just the other side of the rock." Nothing — just the litter of the forest floor. Then, as though a kaleidoscope had shifted: the back and tightly tucked wings of a grouse, lying dead, not ten feet in front of me. Except it was not dead. The head was up, utterly immobile. All the bird's life was concentrated in her eye, which gleamed directly into mine.

This was early May, the rivers still cold and high, the leaves still furled, the sunlight soft on the soft ground. No rain in the forecast. By next week, the rivers would be ready, with the early mayflies — Hendricksons — emerging, and we would come back. But for now we — John Cullen, Fred Scholz, and I — were just getting the camp set for another fishing season. John had been about to fell a big poplar hanging over the driveway when he somehow spotted the hen on her nest. Over the next two days, we looked in on her occasionally. Her position and posture never varied, not by an inch.

They had not varied when we returned the following week, but before we left again, three days later, she had realigned herself by perhaps 10 degrees. The fishing gave us every reason to return the week after. The leaves were unfurling; the ridges that rose across the river from our ridge showed a delicate haze of lime and sage greens and pale pewter grays. Things would change fast now, but the grouse was just as we had left her, a consolidation of leaf litter with an eye shining out of it.

The fishing was good again this time — better than good, in fact. So, we returned for a third straight week. The leaves were bigger, the understory of the woods darker. A fern that had un-furled just beside her nest and the little ash, leafed out now, formed a canopy. I had to step closer, and yet closer, then I found the admonitory eye, barely visible between the fern frond and the overhanging ash. Not a blink, not the least cringing down: *This is a serious matter*, the eye said. *Pretend you never saw me.*

Next time, I found an empty depression, marked by broken eggshells. She and the chicks were scouring the woods now; at night, they'd snuggle under her. Later in June, I came across an-other brood — half-sized fledglings, capable of fluttering flight. By mid-July, I sometimes saw families dust-bathing along the logging roads, all of a size now.

Back in the spring, there was coyote scat along the camp driveway. No shortage of foxes and weasels in that neighborhood either, or of goshawks. Red squirrels are always everywhere: in-doors, outdoors, busy-bodied, prying, and by no means averse to omelets. How often death must have padded within a few feet of the incubating hen, scampered up the spruce behind her,or perched, in the dire, stoop-shouldered form of a goshawk, on a branch over her head. She could not look up or flinch — only sit there, a statue with a living eye.

The May fishing that year was the best I've had, ever. The ensuing summer was satisfactory, before tapering off in August. In September, fish prepare to push up into skinny streams to spawn — another high-risk reproductive strategy. Before they do, they gather in certain places along the river, and some of them are big. With luck, we catch one of those, then return it gently to the water, playing God. The shadows are long, the leaves are turning. Soon, that fish will roll the dice, bet the house, and go into water where no fish belongs.

Those rivers, those woods, those fleeting seasons in which flesh, fish, and fowl are begotten, born, and die. "No country for old men," the poet tells us. He's dead wrong.

SEPTEMBER 2018

Driving through Maine, you sooner or later pass under high-tension wires. On either side of the road, big clear-cut corridors — the interstate highways of the power grid — stretch over hill and dale, highway and river, carrying the electricity that keeps us humming. On the pylons that hold the wires aloft, you occasionally see an osprey nest — a shabby mess of sticks and twigs, compared to which a rat's nest is a Grecian Urn.

Ospreys antedate *homo sapiens* by many thousand millennia. Like us, they inhabit every continent and subcontinent except Antarctica. Unlike us, they are antisocial specialists. They catch fish in shallow water. It's always worked for them. But fifty years ago, they seemed destined for oblivion. Then, in 1972, the EPA outlawed the lethal pesticides that had drastically reduced ospreys' reproductive success, and the Clean Rivers Act became law, reviving the fisheries in many rivers and bays that the birds depended on. The population rebounded with surprising speed and vigor. Which caused a new problem: a shortage of suitable nesting sites along our highly developed waterfronts.

The birds solved this one themselves. They nested on bridge girders, navigational buoys, pilings, piers, and transmission towers. As for us, they tolerated our proximity but did not look for handouts. They raised their young, and then, although monogamous and the best of parents, resumed their solitary lives — migrating down to South America alone, overwintering alone, returning to their nests alone the next spring. And fishing, fishing, fishing, all the way there and all the way back.

A CMP power corridor forms the southern boundary of our property. Early last April, a pair of ospreys — newlyweds, so to speak — built themselves a nest there. Every so often, we'd see one or the other of them flying over the yard, trailing a 2- or 3-foot stick behind it, like a kite's tail. I'd walk over to the corridor from time to time and check on their progress.

The structure they'd chosen consisted of three uprights of laminated wood, standing in a row, like goalposts set 70 feet apart, with an additional goalpost halfway between them. Two parallel timbers, bolted to each other through the tops of the uprights, constituted the crossbar. Each timber looked to be about six inches square — an inch or two wider than a gymnast's balance beam. The gap between them was a little wider than they were.

The tops of the beams, where the nest was materializing, were, I reckoned, 80 feet above the ground. The view from there would be terrific; so would the wind. The "nest" that took shape was simply a thin mat of sticks, laid haphazardly across the beams and the gap between them. I expected the wind to make short work of it.

But it didn't, and I eventually saw why. Besides the through-bolts that held the crossbars to the uprights, there were two pairs of heavy bolts across the gaps between the cross beams — to stiffen the whole structure, I suppose. The bolts were set several inches below the tops of the beams. The nest was centered over one of these pairs of bolts — they were, in effect, its floor joists, creating something between a cellar and a foundation for the center of the nest, which was built up from it to spread out over the beams.

Standing under their nest, looking down the power corridor through my binoculars, I could see an older osprey nest on the far side of the river. It was in the identical place, on an upright and crossbeam arrangement identical to the one over my head: about a third of the way between an outer post and the center one. If I were young, I'd study this matter, study every type of pylon that had an osprey nest in it, and study the architecture of every nest. As it is, I'll just have to think about it.

OCTOBER 2018

In late September, the sun passes into Libra, the Scales, where it spends most of October. Libra is the only zodiacal sign represented by a man-made object: a simple balance beam, once an everyday tool for weighing and measuring things, keeping us honest with each other and ourselves. The blindfolded goddess Justice traditionally held such a beam in her right hand.

Libra begins just after the autumnal equinox, when daylight balances darkness. Throughout the northern hemisphere, the season of harvest is underway: we sell our crops, settle our debts, and reap as we have sown. In the Northeast, the Red Sox and the Yankees head down the home stretch, their seasons hanging in the balance. In America, Election Day — our secular and biennial Judgment Day — bears down upon us.

By October, students and teachers have settled into the business of measuring and weighing, grading and compiling the records by which they will be judged and ranked. Slowly and imperfectly, the wheat is being separated from the chaff, the swift from the slow. For my grandchildren, the process is just beginning. For me, it is essentially over: the hay is in the barn, the final scorecard has been turned in, and the account is closed. Viewed with detachment, my CV doesn't contain much worth bragging about or much to be ashamed of.

For all my fifty years in Maine, May and October have been the most vivid and anticipated months of the year. Judging and being judged, building up my résumé or my bank balance, have never seemed less important; simply being alive on this earth, in this place and at these seasons, has never seemed more so.

My usual vantage point in October has been Merrymeeting Bay. Wild rice ripens and withers; the maple swamps blaze red, then stand bareheaded, a stark and steely gray. Waterfowl arrive; stripers, alewives, and herring depart. Hunting — the oldest profession? — has always been the pretext for my being on the bay and vice versa. In October, when I was still teaching, I would be conscious of the lunar and tidal cycles and the times of sunrise and sunset even as I sat in my office, duly diligent. The clock ticked, deadlines loomed, and midterms approached. W.H. Auden's wonderful phrase, "Find the mortal world enough," ran in my mind then, and not all that business about wheat and tares, sowing and reaping, and publishing while perishing.

Auden, of all poets, understood that we as a species are distinguished by an inability to find the mortal world enough. We create history, record it, endure it, and are responsible to it. Lately, with my Octobers at last free, I've sat on the bay, watching, waiting, and hunting seriously, but also reflecting, not on my own life but on the life of my generation. The best evidence, scrupulously collected and collated, increasingly indicates that we have seen something not seen since the end of the Wisconsin Ice Age: not simply some changes in global climate, but the commencement of a new geological epoch, defined, as the last one was, by drastic relocations of coastlines and the elimination of whole ecosystems and the life that depended upon them. This new epoch, the Anthropocene, will happen with unprecedented rapidity, and be accompanied by unimaginable and compounding demographic, political, and economic calamities.

The legacies of my generation, individual and collective, will be various: much to boast about and much to be ashamed of.

Many of us have raised our children — and they are raising theirs — to tune their ears to the deeper music of the natural world, its seasons and its creatures, things that will continue beneath the cacophony of the human world. But our legacy to them, it appears, will be a world untuned, the scales that blind Justice holds in her right hand unbalanced. In her left hand, the October goddess holds a sword.

NOVEMBER 2018

About twenty years ago, I dreamed a dream. The world lay before me. I could go wherever I pleased, with one exception — I could never again set foot in the Kennebec/Androscoggin watershed. Or I could live there, but on the condition that I never go beyond it. I woke up knowing that, if forced to choose, I'd choose the watershed over the world. The conviction, like the dream, seemed to come from beyond myself.

The Androscoggin and Kennebec converge in Merrymeeting Bay, leave it through a narrow and turbulent passage called the Chops, go down past Bath, and continue on out to sea. Their combined flow represents roughly a third of the running water in Maine. Fifteen or so lesser rivers feed into them, along with more streams, brooks, and springs than you can shake a stick at. Within their drainage are at least forty natural lakes and ponds of more than 1,000 acres and a multitude of smaller ones.

Watershed boundaries are determined by topography, not by surveyors. Everything connects to everything else. From the meltwater on the summit of Old Speck, Sugarloaf, and Saddleback to the tides that surge out past Pond Island Light off Popham Beach, the Kennebec watershed is like a tree: a single organic system, its trunk, branches, twigs, and leaves shaping and shaped by its environment. Long before our species appeared, migratory fish and waterfowl swarmed up and down it; when we arrived, drawn to its abundant life, we did the same. By paddle, pole, and portage, the first people made their way into adjacent watersheds — the Penobscot, the St. Lawrence, and the St.

John — establishing corridors for trade, migration, and invasion. European colonists established themselves in Phippsburg, at the mouth of the river, in 1607 — before the Puritans got to Massachusetts and the Dutch colonized Manhattan.

My dream indicates that I am one kind of provincial, the country mouse. A famed 1975 *New Yorker* cover by illustrator Saul Steinberg gives the perspective of his city cousin. The foreground, a few busy blocks of Manhattan, constitutes its lower half. The upper half consists of America west of the Hudson: an arid wasteland with a few rocks and names — Chicago, Nebraska, Las Vegas — scattered across it. Once you cross the Hudson, America is an uninhabitable Sahara.

If country mice are geographically provincial, city mice are historically provincial. A relation to geological, biological, and human pasts is as optional and inessential to Steinberg's caricatural Manhattanites as my relation to Netflix is to me.

Of course, in Maine, Manhattan, or anywhere else, the choice between the two provincialisms is not so stark as my dream made it. In Vacationland, we — me, you, — don't have to become either antiquarian, contrarian rustics, on the one hand, or cosmopolitan tourists-in-residence — mere consumers of local scenery, local color, and local lobsters — on the other. Most of us are a bit of both.

The Founding Fathers understood that the view from every citizen's window is necessarily local, geographically and/or historically provincial, economically self-serving, and instinctively self-centered. They did not pretend that the situation was otherwise — that we were inherently high minded, idealistic, or patriotic. They devised a government that ensured ongoing political friction between local and national perspectives, so that competing provincialisms would be forced to acknowledge each other and comprehend their mutual dependencies.

This November's midterm elections pit us against each other in ways that seem to have precious little to do with realities grounded in our local and national geographies or their histories. The national map has been simplified at every level: so many Blue states, districts, precincts, and households vs. so many Red ones. There is a strange absence of what we actually see, the neighborhoods and nation we actually inhabit. Is this the view from Trump Tower? From every man's castle? Both?

December 2018

For a couple of weeks back in September, Hurricane Florence made Conway, South Carolina, a famous place for perhaps the first time in its history. In 1999, Hurricane Floyd had been designated a 500-year flood, with the Waccamaw River cresting at 17.7 feet; in 2016, Hurricane Matthew exceeded that by a couple of inches. And now, Florence has exceeded them by better than three feet. In that low, alluvial, swampy country, a foot or two of *superfluous (over + flowing)* water can spread for miles. Was Florence a thousand-year flood event? Ten thousand? Biennial?

I'm an old man, folks; more and more things seem strange to me. Few more so than sitting in Maine and staring at a screen that shows neighborhoods I'd known as a boy standing pooled in their own reflections, the streets as placid as Venetian canals, perhaps with a kayak or canoe paddling down one of them — somebody going home to rescue food from the freezer, or just to survey, for the third time in twenty years, a scene of sheer sodden hopelessness. All that sheetrock to be torn out again, those buckled floors, and mold everywhere, complemented by the sweltering heat, swarming mosquitoes, and on-the-scene reporters that follow hurricanes.

Every summer in the fifty years I've lived up here, there have been a few days sultry and sweaty enough to evoke my boyhood summers. But this summer, we had day after day of that, from July to September and beyond. Finally, that misery broke, and our famous fall arrived — up north, as beautiful a one as I have ever seen. The drama of the year in Maine never gets old because it never slows down; our seasons are strictly migratory, on their way from north to south, from south to north. And as you get older, those seasons accelerate, arriving and departing like houseguests — hardly time to clean up after one before the next one is on the doorstep.

Only in midsummer does the first thin stubble of wild rice appear on the mudflats of Merrymeeting Bay. We hunters of migratory waterfowl watch it the way investors watch the stock market, and in midsummer, we despair, certain that this year's crop will fail. Then we close our eyes, turn around three times, and look again. Presto! At low tide, the flats have suddenly become like lush, silky green fields of oats — the rice more than head high, in some places so thick a dog can't push through it. Close our eyes and turn around three more times, and — anti-presto! — the rice has yellowed, sagged, and lies flat on the mud. Skeins of it form into mats and drift out with the tides. But it has done its work. The flats are seeded — enough for next year's crop, and enough for this year's waterfowl. Soon, skim ice begins forming on the flats at night. The next tide lifts it off, but now, in December, it thickens and sticks, blanketing the flats. The waterfowl depart; their season is ended. Soon, the bay is frozen over and looks like the jumbled ice fields Peary negotiated on his way to the Pole.

Up to Camp

North is merely a direction of travel. It can get you to Maine. But within Maine, *up north* signifies a destination: roughly the upper half of the state, an area bigger than Massachusetts. It contains a few scattered towns. Everything else is officially classified as *unorganized territories* — that is, civic divisions containing too few citizens to have any form of local government. These territories are mostly called townships, but sometimes *grants, public reserved lands, gores*, etc. They were originally laid out with the idea that they would attract colonists, whose settlements would eventually subdivide them into actual towns, thereby peopling the wilderness, improving land, raising property values, and repaying many times over the investment of the original proprietors. Things went according to plan in the lower part of the state. Up north, they did not. Decades passed, then centuries. The townships remained townships, and the region remained a kind of arrested frontier.

So going *up to camp* involves traveling backward as well as northward. To all appearances, history is still waiting to happen there.

I went up north for the first time in 1972. I'd heard promising things about the fishing. I went back a couple of times that year and haven't missed a year since. Mostly, I went with my father, who had just retired. We always stayed in the same inexpensive rental cabin — one room, indoor plumbing, a hotplate to cook on, a small metal table to eat on, a small refrigerator. We left early for fishing, returned for lunch and a nap, then went fishing again.

No DeLorme *Atlas* in those days. The paper companies were still running pulpwood down the river on a daily basis. You drove on their roads — which were rough, narrow, and slow — at your own risk, trying to find your way to some pond that somebody had said was good. Sometimes.

A few times, I went up alone and stayed at a camp belonging to a colleague. He'd owned it for a decade or so and had fished that territory long before that. He knew the country. He'd bought the camp for a song. It was on leased land, and it was dilapidated, dark, stuffy, poorly screened, and beginning to sag. He was perfectly happy with it.

The spruce budworm outbreak in the mid-'70s changed everything all over the north woods. Paper companies began cutting on a much larger scale and building bigger and better roads to get logs to the mills, as though the only way to save the forest was to destroy it. We drove their wider, smoother roads through miles of clear-cut that looked like the Western Front circa 1917. The river drives ended. We kept fishing, learning a little more each year about where to go at what season and how to fish when we got there.

In 1985, without any warning, the lease on my friend's camp suddenly increased tenfold. He'd always known it could happen. He kept his ear to the ground and heard that a fellow was selling off lots on a steep, short road that went up to the top of what was locally known as Hungry Mountain. He and I and four others chipped in $2,000 apiece, bought a 5-acre lot, and proceeded to build a house there, a happy memory in itself. Then we incorporated ourselves, drew up some bylaws, and went fishing.

That was 35 years ago. My father was 78 years old, the age I am right now. He was leery about the camp. It had no plumbing, no electricity. We slept in a bunkroom, on double-decker bunks made out of 2 x 6 lumber left over from the construction. He'd lived in quarters like that in the Marianas during the war, coped with it, and had no wish to repeat it. Two years after he got back to South Carolina, a stranger to his 6-year-old son, he took me fishing. That never stopped — a lot of hours together in a small boat, on a river he'd fished all his life. It kept us close and aware of our differences. Then I moved to Maine. Not long after, he retired, bought a house in Harpswell, spent the summers there, and we went fishing — new waters, new ways of doing it, but within protocols that were second nature to us both. He wasn't sure he wanted to share that.

Camp. The word came into English from French 500 years ago. As a noun, it was a strictly military term: a temporary base for troops sent out on some *camp*aign that separated them from the main body of the army. The place in the Marianas where Daddy spent the war, for example.

Words, individuals, nations, and the earth itself all have histories. They are entangled. Before there were townships or Euro-Americans, there were successive groups of Native people. They lived in *camps* but had no word equivalent to ours, any more than they had a word for unorganized wilderness. Before them, there was the history of geography. Only 17,000 years ago, whales and porpoises frolicked over most of what now consti-

tutes Maine's organized territories. Today's unorganized territories lay under ice a mile thick. Four thousand more years passed
before northernmost Maine was free of ice. By then, the first people had arrived from the south. They found the deepest soils and
richest habitats in the lands that had rebounded from the sea as
the glacier withdrew. The climate and vegetation of northern
Maine approximated what's now found above the Arctic Circle.

The land rebounded further; the forest spread north. Four
great river systems took shape: the Kennebec/Androscoggin, the
Allagash/St. John, the Penobscot, and the St. Croix. The first
three converged to within easy portaging distance of each other
at Moosehead Lake. Successive generations of Native peoples established a network of portages linking rivers, streams, and
ponds, enabling them to go from almost any point in Maine to
almost any other point, also to cross over into the huge St.
Lawrence watershed. The Europeans arrived, expropriated this
system, and used it for their own purposes, the chief of which
was logging, a North American industry hitherto monopolized
by beavers.

Demand for wood was global and insatiable. The supply
in northern Maine appeared unlimited, and the infrastructure
for transporting it down to the mills and ships — the rivers —
was in place. To turn trees into money, all you needed to do was
send an army of men and draft animals into the woods in winter,
provide them with food, fodder, and some sort of shelter until
the thaw came, then shepherd the logs downriver — dangerous
work, but river drivers, like fellers, teamsters, horses, and oxen,
were expendable. It was a vast, logistically complex operation,
utterly analogous to a military *camp*aign. So what were you going
to call the temporary settlements that sprang up like ice-fishing
villages every winter? *Camps*, of course.

Absentee ownership has always prevailed in Maine's unorganized territories. From the beginning, this ran counter to a deeply rooted American assumption that hunters, trappers, and fishermen were free to pursue their quarry whenever, however, and wherever they wished and that unsettled country was a kind of common. Trappers and market hunters presupposed the right to build themselves camps in the Maine woods. Like it or not, the legal owners of those woods, mostly timber companies, learned to live with it — and, as the north woods became more accessible, to profit from it.

Railroads reached the woods, and suddenly tourists and sportsmen represented opportunity. The companies could open lodges and inns or lease land for that purpose. And as a matter of public relations, they permitted the use of their roads to gain access to the north woods' rivers, lakes, and mountains. They leased small parcels of heavily cutover land for modest prices, and they permitted camps, like the one my friend had, to be built on them.

My father came around on the matter of the camp on Hungry Mountain. Usually, when we went up, we'd have it to ourselves, and he'd be relieved. But there came a day when he remarked that he used to be disappointed when we found someone else there ahead of us; now, he was disappointed when there wasn't. I had observed this but hadn't expected him to admit it.

He continued to go up until his last summer, which was 15 years ago. Since then, two of the founding members have died, replaced by people who'd been to the camp as guests and took to its ethos. The building — board and batten, unplaned wood — has weathered into its surroundings. It has no foundations; the joists are spiked to posts that sit on small cement pads. The windows were salvaged from a demolition site; the furniture, small gas stove, woodstove, pots, pans, utensils, sink, etc. all came from various barns and attics. Two 5-gallon water jugs sit under the sink; a 10-gallon jug sits beside it. They represent our plumbing. Fill the smaller jugs at a roadside spring, lug them inside, empty them into the big jug beside the sink. Before you leave, be sure the big jug is topped up, the camp swept out, the kitchen table wiped clean, the trash collected, the gas turned off.

You always leave things as you found them; next time you come up, a week or a month later, no matter who has been up in the interval, you find them as you left them. Unpack. Go fishing. Drive the log roads. Pole the canoe upriver. Get back to camp late. Eat, sleep. Rise early — about 4 a.m. in June. Before you have the coffee started, the first log trucks are rattling and banging along down on the highway, heading up north for the first load of the day. Up north, down south, the same story: *time is money, money is life.* A little after that, tentative at first, a robin, then another. And now, from the low thickets, hermit thrushes up and down the hillside, flute-like and dream-haunting. Reveille. You're up to camp. Rise and shine. Rivers await.

Catch and Release

Remember the summer of 2020? Post-COVID, pre-vaccine. Nobody understood the virus; handwashing and social isolation were the order of the day. On March 15 of that year, Governor Mills announced a state of emergency in Maine. Businesses closed down; tourism dried up.

In camp, new rules: one member at a time, three nights maximum, disinfect all surfaces before leaving. Then, a full day must pass before the next member comes up. All of us are high-risk geezers, burdens upon the Earth but in no hurry to leave it. We have the upper Kennebec and Dead rivers to live for — Kennebec in the mornings, upstream from The Forks; Dead in the evenings, downstream from Grand Falls.

August normally means dry weather, warm water, slow fishing. The summer of 2020 was even drier than usual. Most Augusts, I'd just wait until September, but not that year. My turn came up, and up I went.

Better-than-expected fishing on Friday and Saturday. I poled the canoe up from The Forks, stopping here and there to fish. Caught some, lost some — one big. The Forks itself was a ghost town. The state of emergency had shut down commercial rafting. School buses no longer left the inns and campgrounds every morning, taking rafting parties, guides, and rafts up to Harris Station Dam, at the head of the Kennebec Gorge, so they could go bucking and plunging, whooping and hollering down through the gorge and back to The Forks.

Geezers rise early. On Sunday, August 23, 2020, my last morning in camp, I headed up to fish the gorge at Magic Hole, aka Maytag. Thirty-five years earlier, the year we built the camp, we fished there pretty often. At Maytag, two miles downstream from Harris, high water reached us about 10:30. We'd wade ashore, stand and watch a few rafts come by, some almost back-flipping when they plunged down into Maytag and up the standing wave beyond it. Then, back to camp, a quick lunch and those long, long June afternoons for lugging, measuring, sawing, leveling, spiking, and nailing lumber. Sills, joists, subfloor, floor. Frames, rafters, ridgepole, collar ties, roof. Boards, battens. By mid-July: *Hey! Presto! Fait accompli!* A camp! No electricity! No running water! Furnished out of attics and auction barns! Second-hand mattresses scavenged from Bowdoin College! Live-in mice who look after it when we close for the winter and greet us when we return each spring! Maine! The Way Life Should Be! We were all youngsters then, most of us still in our 40s, which is also The Way Life Should Be.

I went to Maytag that Sunday in 2020 for the same reason we did back in 1985, to abbreviate my fishing time. I'd quit at 10:30, then walk the rim trail back to Carry Brook, where I'd left the truck, and get to camp with plenty of time to eat lunch, nap, clean up, disinfect, and head home to Topsham; be there by suppertime.

At Harris Station, the dam looms up over a pool. Three long flights of steep wooden stairs go down to it. In a normal year, the first busloads of rafters get there a bit before 10. At 9, a siren sounds; early-bird anglers in earshot wade ashore. To warn those out of earshot, the gates on the dam open enough to boost the overnight minimum flow, 340 cubic feet per second, up to 700. If you're standing in the water, you can feel the difference that makes, and you go ashore. As you are getting off the water, the rafters are getting onto it. At 10:00, the dam opens, the flow goes up to 5,000 cfs, and the Kennebec rises four or five feet in a matter of seconds. Generators whir, rafters come bobbing and bouncing down. Your trout river is gone; the cash flow is on.

I had three hours of utterly private and devout fishing — *the Lord is in His holy temple, let all the earth keep silence before Him*, that sort of thing. The mists and freshness of predawn twilight last longer down in the shadow of the gorge. But it's an awkward place to fish: bare rock and trees crowd in behind you; the river in front of you drops off to black depths just a few feet from shore. You plant your wading staff firmly before every step; before every cast, you check to see how much room your backcast will have. And you watch the water in front of you for the dimple of a rising fish or a ghostly mayfly drifting on the current.

I'd managed to catch and release three fat, frisky 12-inch salmon, and it was almost quitting time. Fewer insects were on the water, and fewer fish were rising. But one dimpled the current, just within range. I cast; the fly drifted true and disappeared in a small swirl. I set the hook and *whoa!* A good one, much better than the others. He ran a long way upstream, ripping off line, then reversed direction and came back by me, headed for a run of water a dozen yards downstream from where I stood and close in against the bank. If he got below that run, I wouldn't be able to work him back against the current. I snubbed him up short; he jumped high, twisting and thrashing in midair. The fly flew. Fishermen refer to this as the *LDR* — the Long-Distance Release.

With that excitement over, I felt the current tugging more

insistently at my pant legs. The 700-cfs flow was arriving. No need to hurry. I waded carefully ashore, sat on a rock, uncoupled my rod and put it in its case, took off my heavy wading shoes and laced on ordinary hiking boots. I put the shoes in my landing net, picked up my wading staff, and stood up, ready for the walk back to the truck.

And there, right in front of me, was a whitewater raft, just entering the run of water where I'd lost the salmon. Immediately behind it was another, and another behind that. They were strangely silent — no whooping and hollering. The six paddlers in the closest raft, perched opposite each other on the bolsters, were all business, perfectly erect, eyes fixed on the river, and they were perfectly in sync, paddlers on each side simultaneously digging in hard. The sternman — who, with a raft full of customers, would have been shouting out instructions and switching from side to side with his longer paddle, trying to hold the raft on course — was as silent as his crew, laying back and using his paddle as a steering oar.

I'd never thought much about whitewater guides. I knew that they had to be licensed by the state and that the licensing procedure involved a week of rigorous training, overseen by experienced guides. It always takes place before the summer season has begun. The trainees pay good money to put in very long days. They obtain their licenses only if they demonstrate proficiency in advanced first aid and CPR, plus an ability to cope with all sorts of emergency situations on the river — passengers overboard, rafts hung up on rocks or flipped over entirely, with everyone, including the guide, going into the river, requiring the next raft to rescue them. And they have to know this particular stretch of river, at various stages of water, just as well as a golf pro knows a home course. Both they and their instructors have to discipline their adrenaline-fueled addiction to whitewater but not lose it. I knew all this because two of my friends had undergone this training. One liked it so much that he gave up fishing, guided whitewater-rafting trips on the Kennebec, the Dead, and the Penobscot all summer long, then went down to Chile, taking advantage of the austral summer and making whitewater rafting his career for a few years. The other completed the training to prove to himself that he could, then hung up his wet suit and went back to fishing.

What I did not know was that some years earlier, the rafting guides had begun staging an annual Olympics, open only to their fellow guides. Competitors included those who'd been guiding for years as well as those who'd gotten licenses in the spring, so the event gave instructors and students an opportunity to compete, to measure themselves against each other. These Olympics are always held late in the summer. They are, in part, a valedictory ceremony concluding another season and, in part, a refresher course, but surely the main motive is for guides to get together and have themselves some good, clean, serious, strenuous fun.

I have no idea why the guides chose to stage the Olympics in 2020, after a summer in which there had been no commercial rafting. The Olympics are not a commercial event, so holding them was technically legal. Perhaps doing so was an act of faith or hope (is there any difference?). The guides would have at least one fine memory from that lost summer to tide them over through the winter. As it turned out, my last morning of fishing was on the day they'd chosen for their event.

I stood and watched. Once the lead raft was through the salmon run, it angled across the current, toward the far bank. The trailing rafts followed in a strict line. They looked like middle-distance runners, still in a tight pack, pushing the pace, but no one yet trying to break away. They had materialized unexpectedly, out of nowhere, the way things do in dreams, and the complete silence of their intense and beautiful effort enhanced that effect. Soon, sunlight would touch the river on the far side; already the ranks of pines and firs between the river and the rim of the gorge were glowing in it.

But I had my hike ahead of me. With the rod and landing net in my left hand and the wading staff in my right, I started up the path that leads to the rim. I wanted to be very deliberate about it. The first part runs over a boulder about the size of a VW Beetle, its surface covered with thick moss and stunted firs, and the faint trail skirts the edge overlooking the river. The trail is plenty good enough for goats, suboptimal for geezers. With each step, I planted my staff solidly in the mossy scruff of the downslope, put my weight on it, then looked back down at the rafters. I reflected — I remember this — that they were traveling faster than the flow, because they were paddling. They were in danger of overtaking the bony, bumpy minimum flow just ahead of them or, if they held back, of being overtaken by the avalanche of the cash flow, rushing down from behind. Like the voyage of life, I thought to myself, all wry and philosophic. The first rafts were disappearing around a downstream corner. The cast was going offstage; the show would soon be over.

And then I was sitting, my back against the base of the mossy boulder. I had no memory of having fallen and no consciousness of being injured. But I was having a hard time standing up, and I felt around for my staff. I was not 10 feet from the edge of the river, just upstream from the run of water where the salmon had jumped. And here was a raft heading into the run, the paddlers all in sync, facing downriver. But not the sternman. He was looking directly at me.

I saw him calling out something to the paddlers, then ruddering the raft, so that it angled in toward the shore as it came through the salmon run. It thumped against the bank; I heard the splashing of the crew getting out, and then the sternman — looking stern indeed: bearded, intent — was squatting in front of me. I asked him if he could help me up — I'd had a fall, maybe kinked my knee somehow.

"You're bleeding," he said. "Bleeding a lot."

I later learned that an alert kayaker — also a rafting guide, but kayaking today — had seen me there or possibly seen me as I fell. She — Emily by name — had, as they all had, some sort of fancy shortwave radio, as cell phones don't work down in the gorge. She radioed the sweep raft, the raft that trails all the others, not competing but riding herd on them. If there was trouble — a paddler thrown off the side, a raft hung on a rock — the sweep raft would notify all other rafts ahead, telling them to pull in to shore. Once the problem was resolved, the race would resume. The grave-looking man in the sweep raft, whose face was the first thing I saw, was Alex.

I do not remember his bandaging my head, but it must have been a quick, expert job; no blood got into my eyes. I do remember the six paddlers arriving, carrying a stretcher, putting it down, and lifting me onto it. I lay flat on my back. Perhaps my wrists and ankles were buckled down, to keep me from turning onto my side or trying to sit up. Perhaps they put a neck brace on me. They laid me in the raft, and then we were moving, bobbing along downstream. Once or twice, water splashed over the bow and into my face. I must have been in shock — I felt no pain. I remember laughing and saying that this was pretty good — I was getting a free rafting trip down the river, deluxe service. A paddler said, "Don't forget — we've got your wallet too." That seemed to me very funny.

I remember them pulling into the eddy at Carry Brook, where I'd left the truck, and I remember the rafters carrying my stretcher up the rustic staircase that goes to the top of the gorge. The staircase was familiar to me — I'd occasionally take a canoe down it to float and fish through the lower section of the gorge. At the top of the stairs, they put me into the back of a truck parked just beside mine. They laid some kind of padding under the stretcher and held some more of it down over me, so that I could not bounce or roll — the first few miles of the road were rough. Someone told me that they had radioed ahead to the Skowhegan hospital and that an ambulance was being dispatched northwards. I'd be transferred to it. That seemed to make sense, although I felt no pain, had no other awareness of being seriously hurt. As the truck bounced along, I think I remember some friendly conversation about fishing and rafting, but I cannot be sure.

From that point on, I apparently faded in and out of consciousness. No recollection of being transferred from truck to ambulance or from ambulance to the Skowhegan hospital. Distinct memory of a CAT scan, an MRI, and X-ray in the Skowhegan hospital, and of someone faceless — wearing a surgical mask, perhaps off to one side, out of my field of vision — telling me the results, and that I would be transferred to Maine Medical Center, in Portland. But no memory of that ambulance trip either.

Maine Med was a rerun of Skowhegan. My memory resumes with me on my back, on a stainless-steel table: a CAT scan, an MRI, an X-ray. A voice — technician, doctor, physician's assistant? — told me exactly what I'd been told in Skowhegan: I had cracked my skull, fractured the second vertebra in my neck, broken my right clavicle, my sternum, a rib, and damaged several vertebrae in my tailbone. Plus a lot of scalp wounds, which accounted for all the bleeding. The voice said everything looked fine and prophesied a complete recovery. But apart from the voice, the prophesy, and those machines, I might as well have been laid out for an autopsy. My memory of the experience resembles the residue of nightmares: the same sense of powerlessness, of being both a participant and an observer.

Then, I awoke to find myself lying on a hospital bed at Maine Med, in Portland, flat on my back, wearing a rigid neck brace. From that point on, time resumed its ordinary continuity, except for the fact that I slept through so much of it. After a day or so in the hospital, I was taken a few blocks to a rehab center and spent a couple of weeks there. Every four hours, I was given pain pills; they worked for three hours. The brace kept me staring straight ahead, like a Buckingham Palace guard. I was not to lie on my side — doctor's emphatic orders. I could press a button and the hospital bed would convert into something like a lounge chair, so that I could eat my meals, watch television — a wall-mounted set, up near the ceiling — and read for a few pages, holding the book stiff-armed out in front of me. Susan brought from home Richard Ford's collection of stories, *Sorry for Your Trouble*. What could be more apropos?

Every afternoon, the therapist came, raised the bed so I could sit up, lowered the side rail, and helped me swing my legs over and put my feet on the floor. As I stood up, she held one of those four-legged walkers for me to grasp, and we shuffled out of the room, across the hall, and into the therapy room. It was a cheerful place, sunlight coming in through large windows along one wall and with furnishings and a general ambience that suggested a day-care center. There might be as many as eight or 10 other patients with their therapists. Most of us were old, but we resembled toddlers as we did our exercises, wobbly on our feet, pushing walkers ahead of us or side-stepping along a counter, using our hands for balance or, with banisters on both sides to hold, laboring — half walking, half pulling ourselves — up a gently inclined plane or a short flight of low steps. Gerontology recapitulating phylogeny: we were evolving into bipeds all over again.

Susan came daily, sometimes with one of our daughters. They would stand at the foot of the bed or lean over it, so I could see them. They were emissaries from the real, whole, and solid world: Bowdoinham, Topsham, and The Way Life Should Be. Finally, one day, I was led out into the warm sunshine of a September morning, maneuvered from the walker into a van, and taken home.

A year and a half later: February 28, one week shy of my 80th birthday and time for my annual physical examination, preceded by the usual routine lab work. When he had first agreed to become my primary caregiver, the doctor had been a young man, his children barely of school age. Those children were now in college or the early stages of medical school; he was in the prime of life. Over the years, my health never gave us much to talk about. By luck of the genetic draw, I had an excellent metabolism, a sound skeleton, freedom from chronic disorders, addictions, allergies, etc. The consequences of such minor mishaps and surgeries as I from time to time incurred were dealt with by physical therapy, and I had become, and remain, a great believer in it. As I reached my mid-70s, I began noticing some slowing down, but when I grumbled about it, the doctor would almost laugh: "Look, regardless of age, you're the healthiest person I'll see this week. This month."

I had left the Maine Med rehab center and returned home in September of 2020. For the first few weeks at home, I spent most of my time just as I had at Maine Medical Center — flat on my back, in a rented hospital bed. I still used the walker to move around the house. Three days a week, physical therapists from the local health-care agency visited. They concentrated on strengthening my legs, improving my balance, and so gradually emancipating me from the walker. I soon could ride in the car. That was a pure treat; I looked forward to it like a dog looking forward to its walk. But driving was still out of the question, as the neck brace allowed me only forward vision. As a passenger, my view was limited to the road ahead, the sidewalks, and road shoulders. The vistas of field and forest, rivers, marshes, and bays were beyond my scope.

Twice a month, Susan drove us to Portland, back to Maine Med. I would have my weight and vital signs checked, then new X-rays would be taken — first, of the rib cage, sternum, and clavicle, which the orthopedist would go over with us, then of the neck and skull, for our appointment with the neurologist. The broken bones mended quickly, the neck and spinal column more slowly. But just before Christmas of 2020, four months after my fall, the neurologist looked at the X-rays and said I need not wear the neck brace any longer. We had not expected to hear that. Hearing it made me feel, if not quite like Prometheus Unbound, then at the very least like Fido Unleashed, free to run and caper and investigate every pissing post in sniffing distance, chase cats, howl at the moon, whatever.

But not so fast. Fido was no frisky young pup. I'd lost fourteen pounds over the past four months, nearly a tenth of my body weight. That didn't make me any skinnier, only flabbier — the lost weight consisted of atrophied muscle. The brace had borne most of the weight of my head; it had also affected my posture. I'd had virtually no exercise involving my torso, neck, shoulders, or arms. So when the brace came off, I was referred to a PT and sports-medicine clinic in Brunswick, with instructions that I undergo "gentle manual therapy and progressive upper back and shoulder strengthening." Progress was incremental but real. I regained at least some of the lost strength, weight, and flexibility. Since the PT ended, I've continued doing exercises at home — an hour each morning, another hour each evening. An old dog, unable to get up to his old tricks, still has his doggedness.

And so, when I saw my primary caregiver, the week before my 80th birthday, he looked me over, pushed and prodded, and asked how I was doing. I had complaints. Walking on even ground, I still felt a kind of stiffness and constraint, as though wearing an inflexible corset; on uneven ground, I was likely to lurch and had trouble stepping over obstacles in my path without stumbling. And my mind encountered similar impediments — getting from point A to point B, finding the right word or the right way to spell it, and following my own logic, whether in writing or conversation, had become slow, errant, and laborious.

The conclusion was that I was still healthy for someone of my age and, by octogenarian standards, sound of mind, memory, and body. The accident had perhaps accelerated the aging process; the best way to deal with it was to go on doing what I was doing — remaining physically and mentally active to the best of my ability.

I have done this — rearguard actions against an opponent who never loses. At night, out of old habit, I try to remember long poems I once knew perfectly well and recited to myself as a way to occupy my mind when I could not sleep. Now, I stumble over the opening stanzas. At other times, fragments surface from poems I'd read long ago and not thought about for decades. Especially this one.

> *This shaking keeps me steady. I should know.*
> *What falls away is always. And is near.*
> *I wake to sleep, and take my waking slow.*
> *I learn by going where I have to go.*

Theodore Roethke wrote that in 1953. I read it eight years later, as a freshman in college. Then, it fell away, buried under the muchness of life. And now is near, once again something I should know. Nothing seems wiser, more descriptive of the place in which, by falling head-first off a rock in the Kennebec Gorge, or simply by being 80 years old, I find myself. Not exactly The Way Life Should Be, but the way it is.

The weeks and months after August 23, 2020, were eventful in the larger world. With remarkable speed, effective vaccines were developed, distributed, and administered. By the summer of 2021, the inns and campgrounds at The Forks were full again, and the rafting business had resumed. That fall, there was a presidential election, followed two months later by an invasion of our national capitol building, a coup attempt that failed. After those things, there was actually a period — do you remember it? — when we talked confidently of things Getting Back to Normal.

Never such innocence again. Now, we must speak resignedly of the New Normal — the very idea of something called Normality having gone the way of hoop skirts and crinolines, top hats, shoeshine boys, Norman Rockwell, and Malkin's maidenhead. In politics, as in epidemiology, we'd placed our faith in herd immunity, underestimating COVID's capacity for generating new versions of itself and overestimating our national capacity for consensus, for agreeing to any version of the recent past that would allow us to move beyond it.

Up in camp this year, new protocols. All of us are vaxxed to the max. And this year, each of us self-administer the COVID antigen test before going up. We hope these precautions, part of the New Normality, will allow us to enjoy something like the old, relaxed conviviality of camp life.

As for the events of that August 23: I still have no recollection of the actual fall. It seems to have happened offstage, although my memories from just before and just after it are exceptionally distinct. The only general precept that seems to apply to what happened that day is that fortune favors fools — and favors them so outrageously that it seems supernatural, an act of God. Providence provided me with the Kennebec River rafting guides, whose training had equipped them to deal with just such an emergency and whose rafts and expertise made them the best — in fact the only — means for a medevac operation from the gorge. And Providence provided them with a test of their skill, training, alertness, and readiness of mind better than any they could have possibly expected or devised — a real emergency, not a simulated one. All the king's horses, all the king's men, all the skill and diligence of all the medical professionals — doctors, lab technicians, physical therapists — would have been unavailing had they failed to deal so expertly with a serious accident in a seriously inconvenient place. All of this, so that, two years after the fact, I might sit comfortably in my chair, on a perfect summer afternoon, and tell you about it.

Tonight, I will lay me down to sleep. Tomorrow morning, please God, I will wake, take the antigen test and, barring an unexpected result, head up to The Forks 15 minutes later. The truck sits in the driveway outside my window; the canoe and the canoe pole are lashed to it. The old dog has his unfailing trick. He can still illustrate an old normality. It has been with us for 25 or 30 centuries. In the days of my youth, my elders quoted it at me as an admonition. Or maybe a prophecy? *As the dog returneth to its vomit, so the fool returneth to his folly* (Proverbs 26:11–13).

Semper Habemos

Convocation Address to the class of 2001, Bowdoin College, September 1997

The class of '01 has been bombarded with facts and stories about the college's past, its buildings, and even some of its trees. This will be the last installment of the bombardment.

I want to talk about the Bowdoin Pines, this church, and a typical college classroom, and then to talk about a book.

The Bowdoin Pines stand beside the Bath Road, a few hundred yards east of us. They are bounded by the gracious houses of Federal Street on one side, and by Darling's Auto Parts on the other. The pines are not as old as the college, but they are big, fine trees, because the college at some point decided not to cut them down and turn them into lumber. It chose instead to make them a symbol of itself. It calls its Alumni newsletter "The Whispering Pines," and somewhere along the line somebody gave the newsletter, and the college, a Latin motto: *pinos loquentes semper habemos* — the whispering pines we shall always have with us.

I think the *we* in the motto does not refer to us here at Bowdoin. In fact, the pines are rather awkwardly located, in an out-of-the-way corner, and not many of us go into them from one year to the next. I think the *we* refers to the alumni, in whose imaginations a quiet grove of trees, sighing softly in the wind, serves as a metaphor — a sort of unconscious poetry — for their youth and their college experience. This association of distant happiness and contemplative innocence is very ancient, present in the myth of Eden and in the Groves of Academos, a wealthy Athenian who owned an estate outside the city. Our word *Academy* originates there, as does the green and leafy ambience of campuses like Bowdoin's. So, our whispering pines are local versions of a cultural archetype, created by nostalgia.

The first Europeans in North America, trying to give an adequate impression of the towering forests they found here, rather frequently compared entering them to entering the hushed gloom of a Gothic cathedral. This church, built by Richard Upjohn in 1846, deliberately evokes the architecture of such a cathedral, and it gives you some sense of what the first Europeans were talking about. If you let your eye follow the columns upward, to the intricate framework of beams and rafters that supports the roof, and consider all the airiness and openness above you, you can begin to imagine yourself as being beneath the canopy of a very stylized and regimented grove of trees. Sitting in this and other churches of its approximate design, I have sometimes wished that more were done to enhance this forest-like quality. Think how pleasant it would be to sit there if the church had been stocked with squirrels, to scamper and frolic through the rafters while the service went on below. Or what would be gained if the windows were permanently open, so that birds might come and go freely. Instead of barn swallows, we would have church swallows, sweeping in through the windows, twittering, building their nests and feeding their young. Parishioners who did not trust entirely to the efficacy of prayer could be provided with umbrellas.

Our beginning this academic year in this church is an anachronism, a ceremonial vestige of what was once an intimate relation between theology and higher education. Our business lies across the street, in the labs and libraries and classrooms. Bowdoin's classrooms are typical of classrooms in general. The great majority of them are basically the same room that the great majority of us entered when we were five or six years old and stay in, for nine months a year, right through elementary and secondary school, and on through any subsequent schooling. Some of us (he said ruefully) have never escaped. The basic design is so familiar and ubiquitous that you hardly notice or think about it — the rows of desks, the blackboard, the overhead lighting that banishes all shadows. No nooks, crannies, or irregularities. They are as predictable and uninteresting in their way of connecting form to function as squash courts or parking lots.

There are paradoxes and contradictions built into churches and classrooms. What goes on in a classroom is intended to liberate the mind, to encourage inquiry, debate, dissent — a freedom, variety, and mobility of thought. But the actual classroom, as a space, does not seem to imply that purpose. It is enclosed, calculated to focus and restrict attention. The desks, the blackboards, the shadowless light, the lack of idiosyncrasy of design all seem to suggest orthodoxy and consistency, as though the aim were to turn out a uniform, standardized product. A squirrel, a bird, or a vagrant thought would be drastically out of place.

With churches, the paradox runs the other way. They were built as places where doctrines were to be expounded. Their aim was not to inspire discussion but assent, a subordinating of the individual personality, will, and intellect to the omnipotence and omniscience of God. But the interior of a church like this one inspires solitary rumination and invites you into yourself. It is very different from the tensed attention and surveillance of the classroom.

I am speaking of churches and churchgoers as a respectful unbeliever, but I think I am speaking of something that even believers experience as they sit through the service. About halfway down the left-hand aisle of this particular building there is a plaque on a pew. Richard Upjohn did not put it there. The plaque commemorates the fact that, while attending communion here on a cold winter's Sunday in 1851, Harriet Beecher Stowe had a vision of a slave being flogged, and then of the same slave on his death's bed. That vision led directly to her writing of *Uncle Tom's Cabin* — the most famous American novel of its time, and the most politically potent novel of our history. I do not believe she could have had this experience if she'd been sitting in one of Bowdoin's classrooms across the street.

The book I want to talk about seems to me to deal profoundly with the issues of education, and with the strange co-dependency of liberation and confinement. It is *The History of Rasselas, Prince of Abyssinia,* by Samuel Johnson. Don't be misled by that word "history" — the story is pure fiction. Johnson wrote in in 1859. He had never been to Abyssinia in his life — not many Europeans had. But a good many French and English writers had written fanciful accounts of it.

All of these accounts agreed that the ancient kings of Abyssinia had confined their children in a place where they would be safe from attack or political intrigue. In some accounts, the place was austere, almost like a prison; in others It was like a high-class resort, offering every amenity and pleasure. It was clearly this latter conception that fired Johnson's imagination.

His story opens in the Happy Valley, a beautiful, secluded spot surrounded by impassable mountains, and accessible only through a single, closely-guarded gate. Here the royal offspring live out their lives, in the company of carefully selected companions of their own age, and of older men and women who can instruct and entertain them, give them access to the highest achievements of the wide and wicked world of human history.

This basic idea of an enclosed place, a walled garden that excludes all evil and contains all the blessings of nature and civilization lay at the heart of Johnson's culture, and it echoes in our own imaginings — the pines that whisper to the nostalgic alumni are one version of it. Johnson's description of the Happy Valley owes a good deal to Milton's description of Eden, which deepens our sense of it as being less a particular place than a generic ideal.

Naturally, the Happy Valley is famous throughout the length and breadth of Abyssinia, and everybody aspires to live there. But only the wisest and most gifted citizens are permitted to apply for admission, either as companions for the royal children or as their instructors and entertainers; and only the very best of these are chosen.

Rasselas, as a Prince of Abyssinia, has inhabited the Valley from birth, enjoying every advantage and free from every worry. When the story opens, he is 26 years old, and has recently been overcome by restlessness and depression, and taken to moping around by himself. We learn that there are two drawbacks to the Happy Valley, although you would have to live there to recognize them as such. The first is that no one is permitted to leave, but why would anyone want to? Why not live under the whispering pines forever? The second is that in the Happy Valley, every good and wholesome pleasure, every delightful entertainment, is perpetually available, there for the asking. All you have to do is to enjoy yourself, hour after hour, day after day, year after year. Rasselas has come to find this intolerable. "I have already enjoyed too much," he says; "give me something to *desire*!"

One day, Rasselas encounters Imlac, an older man famed

for wisdom, and a recent inductee into the Happy Valley. Rasselas questions him about the world outside, and Imlac tells him the story of his life. It has been an admirable life — he has travelled widely, read deeply, and gained great learning and great renown. In the process, he found the world to be a place of delusion, pettiness, and disappointment, and so at last he applied to the Happy Valley and was admitted. Rasselas presses him closely — has the Happy Valley brought him the happiness he craved? Imlac confesses that it has not, and that he, and all the other men and women who have gained admission, secretly rue the day they decided to leave the world and retire there.

So Imlac and Rasselas resolve to escape, and so they do. They are joined by Rasselas' beloved sister, the princess Nekayah, and her handmaiden, Pekuah. Rasselas brings with him enough money to allow them to travel comfortably, and to ensure that all doors will be open to them.

They do not travel as tourists but as investigators. Like any young people, Rasselas and his companions seek a vocation — a life's calling — for themselves. They are not concerned about whether the calling is a prestigious one. It has only to satisfy their wish to live a live that will bear examination, that will seem worthy, significant, and complete.

They investigate courts and cities; they experiment with living among unsophisticated shepherds, tending their flocks, and among the idle rich. They listen carefully to the eloquence of philosophers, visit a hermit in his cave and an astronomer in his tower. They compare the situations of those who have chosen to marry with those who have remained single, of those who have devoted themselves to the pursuit of truth with those who have lived for pleasure.

In all of this, Rasselas finds an outward variety and novelty that at first delight him; but closer examination reveals, over and over again, an inward sameness. Over and over again, he encounters echoes of the restlessness, the feelings of futility, and the sense of confinement that had oppressed him in the Happy Valley; he finds even the most honorable and reflective people to be haunted by a happiness that they have never known, or to fall victim to delusions of grandeur.

Finally, the four sit down and take stock. What are they to do with their lives? At first, they fantasize and idealize. Pekua says that she will devote herself to piety and contemplation, and join a convent. Nekayah opts for education — she will master all the arts and sciences, and then, in an appropriately quiet and sheltered place, will found a college. Rasselas will start his own kingdom, an example to the world of a just and rational society. Their choices have in common the theme of escape, of voluntary confinement in an enclosed, stringently regulated world. Imlac says that he will continue to live as they have been living, travelling, observing, and trying not to expect more from life than life can deliver.

Even in announcing these plans, each of them knows that the plans will come to nothing. They have seen convents and colleges and utopian experiments, and seen how they invariably frustrate or betray the impulses that establish them. And at the same time they know that their role as roving spectators of life is also unsatisfactory, and leaves them with a sense of emptiness.

In the end, they return to the Happy Valley.

Johnson's title for this final chapter is "The Conclusion, in which Nothing is Concluded." If you read the book as a handbook, a guide to choosing your career or your lifestyle, its inconclusive conclusion will seem like a cop-out. It leaves you like Rasselas — sadder and no wiser than you were when you started out.

Instead of conclusions or consolations, *The History of Rasselas* offers only irony. Much of it, I am afraid, is directed against educators and intellectuals. We see how often their lives contradict their teachings, and how great a role competitive egotism and vanity play in the desire to instruct. Even Imlac, a teacher of true humility and wisdom, cannot save Rasselas and the others from false hopes and disappointments. Nor can he be said to learn from his own experience — he has fled from the world to the Happy Valley, realized his mistake, fled back to the world, realized his mistake, and fled back to the Happy Valley — a choice he will presumably live to regret again.

But the irony is strangely sympathetic. Very few of the many characters from many walks of life in Rasselas are fools. Most are candid, thoughtful, and articulate. They say things that all of us, on either side of the podium, would do well to remember, in the middle of our educational endeavors. Things like *Nothing will ever be done if all possible objections to it must first be overcome.* Or *I am inclined to conclude that we grow more happy as our minds take on a wider range.* Or *We differ from ourselves just as we differ from each other.* Johnson's own voice, and his own difficult life, resound in many of the things his characters say. For example: *Of all whom you saw so merry last night, there was not one who did not dread the moment when solitude shold deliver him to the tyranny of reflection.* Or *The truth is, that no mind is much employed upon the present: recollection and anticiplation fill all our moments.* Or *Whoever has no one to love or trust has little to hope.* Or especially this chilling one: *Perhaps if we speak with rigorous exactness, no human mind is in its right state.* These insights do no save the characters; they can diagnose the human condition, but cannot prescribe a cure.

Toward the end of the book, Imlac takes them to see the Great Pyramid of Cheops. They enter the pyramid and sit in its darkest, inmost chamber. The huge, intricate structure has no discernible function, no practical purpose. *It seems to have been erected* Imlac says, *only in compliance with that hunger of imagination which preys incessantly upon human life and must always be appeased by some employment.*

If I were to boil this whole book down to a phrase, this would be it: *That hunger of imagination which preys incessantly upon human life, and must always be appeased by some employment.* Colleges and churches, no less than pyramids, were erected in compliance with that hunger, to give it form and structure, to appease it by employment. But you can look at the confining structure of theological creeds or college classrooms and feel that, while hunger of imagination may have created them, they are now dedicated to disciplining it out of existence — into mere high-minded conformity.

We are just about to cross the street, and in a day or two, we will be in the thick of it — schedules, syllabuses, assignments, deadlines, examinations. Life can be hectic, and if you pause for a moment and look around you, you can begin to wonder if, to speak with rigorous exactness, any mind in this entire community, particularly including your own, is altogether in its right state. What the College View Book represents as an academically accredited version of the Happy Valley begins to feel like boot camp. The imagination becomes preoccupied by fantasies of escape, the hunger for a "Real World" that is by definition elsewhere, and that will confer upon life the satisfying drama and significance of a book or movie.

All of us — parents, teachers, students, administrators — assume that the demanding, strenuous enterprise of liberal arts education enables a new generation to find a place in the world and make its way. That assumption sustains the college, justifying the huge investment of money and effort that it requires. At the same time, we continue to claim that our purposes are not primarily pre-professional, and our curriculum largely supports that claim. When asked to define these broader purposes, most of us, myself included, grow rather vague, and fall back on fancy platitudes.

Speaking only for myself, I think the vagueness comes from the sense, which I have tried to describe, that there is a paradoxical relation between the ends and means of education — its liberating aspirations and its confining realities — and that to experience this paradox in an intense way is the beginning of wisdom. As a student, I experienced, but could not articulate, the ways in which my imagination both fled and craved confinement, both yearned for the relief of self-expression and feared the labor to which it would sentence me, and the very real possibility that the labor would come to nothing. As a teacher, I vacillate between academic stringency, on the theory that imagination, like steam, develops usable energy only when it is pent up almost to the point of explosion; and academic leniency, on the theory that the imagination, like any complex organism, requires time and space in which to grow.

Writing eventually turned out to be the employment by which I undertook to appease the hunger of imagination. I have often wished that I had made some other choice, and have looked, Rasselas-like, with an idealizing envy at ornithologists doing field work, or sculptors and painters in their studios, chemists in their labs, or cabinet-makers or boat-builders in their shops, all savory with the smell of wood. George Orwell says that writing a book is like a long bout with some painful illness. Samuel Johnson must have felt the same way — he was forever accusing himself of postponing writing by doing what we all do when a paper is due — seeking out company, diversion, conversation, or fiddling around the room, or simply sleeping the morning away. Writing was clearly a claustrophobic experience for him — the moment when solitude delivered him to the tyranny of reflection, and to the fear that his own mind was not altogether in its right state. But he always came back to it — he could never not write. In that sense, everything he wrote was inconclusive, since it was going to be followed by something else. For that we may be grateful. Much of his greatness as a writer and a human being grew from his struggle against his own vocation.

A sentence, a paragraph, a page, a book is an enclosed and narrow space, and even within it syntax and idiom are policed by a hodgepodge of logic and custom. To write, or indeed to read in the fully committed way that is necessary to complete the act of writing, requires you to *sentence* yourself to a sort of solitary confinement — to throw the book at yourself, so to speak. This act of self-incarceration can open up worlds, and let light and fresh air into the dark, dank space that lies between the ears. I do not think that writing and reading are unique, in this regard. I think that they, like the great pyramid of Cheops, are monuments to the strange struggle, which neither side can afford to win, between hunger of imagination and the finite circumstances of existence.

Hunger of imagination will not be uppermost in your mind when you walk into the library, around exam time, and find that it is full of people bent over their work, and you are likely to think of panic, determination, ambition, emulation, and anxiety. But I believe that hunger of imagination, moving beyond daydream and fantasy, and now beginning to respond to and react against its strict confinement, gives the scene its highest possibility and best justification.

In reading and writing, you sometimes stop and look at words, and remind yourself that they are relics, with a deep evolutionary past buried within them. Etymologists speculate that *book* is connected to the Old English *boc*, the name for the beech tree, which had a smooth bark suitable for inscription. *Library* comes from *liber*, the pliant underbark of a tree, which the Romans used as an early form of paper. *Paper* itself, although its etymology takes us back to the papyrus reeds of ancient Egypt, is now manufactured from wood pulp, and so a library like Bowdoin's is a vast forest in digest form. We go there to *leaf* through the pages of a journal; we do not graze but *browse* in the stacks.

The whispering pines are awkwardly located, on the other side of campus. They are also, as something between a promise and a memory, always with us. Even here, where Stowe had her vision; even now, in this present with which our minds are so seldom occupied.

Second Growth

My book Confluence *received the John Burroughs Medal for nature writing in 2007. The JBM jury is small, and consists entirely of former winners of the award. John Burroughs himself, a revered and beloved octogenarian, died in 1921; the first award was given, under the sponsorship of the John Burroughs Society, in 1926. It has been given annually in all but 10 of the ensuing years.*

I n the beginning was Thoreau, who laid down the law: "All I ask of any writer, first or last, is a simple and sincere account of his own life, and not merely what he has heard of other men's lives; but some such account as he would send to his kindred, from a distant land, for if he has lived sincerely, it must have been in a distant land to me."

This comes from the opening paragraph of *Walden*, a book that proves it isn't always easy to follow your own advice. It is anything but a simple book; it constantly brings Thoreau's reading—his second-hand knowledge of other men's lives—to bear on his experience; and you can never be sure when he is being sincere and when he is pulling your leg. He is a strange man to have founded a literary tradition, his disdain for such traditions not coincidentally resembling Jesus Christ's disdain for organized religion, and confronting his would-be disciples with similar

119

paradoxes, perhaps the chief of which is this: how do we follow anyone who so urgently encourages us to get lost?

Publishers do not think of the kinfolk back home as the ideal target audience. They want one that is at least regional, preferably national, possibly even global — and that is born again every minute. Thoreau gained no such audience in his own lifetime; John Burroughs, his first (and somewhat conflicted) literary disciple did, and publishers and readers began to recognize the literary and economic possibilities of something called American Nature Writing.

Until six weeks ago, when I received an entirely unanticipated telephone call, I had thought of nature writing as being a bunch of books, some of which I had read and none of which I had written.

If I had been a novelist or poet, and had gotten such a phone call, I wouldn't have felt this way. I would have always known that I was a novelist or a poet and been able to talk more or less sensibly about the novelists or poets, dead or alive, whom I held nearest and dearest. But I do not have that kind of relation to the tradition of nature writing, or at least it never occurred to me that I did until I got the phone call. I felt something of the startled delight of Moliere's Monsieur Jourdain, who learned that, unbeknownst to himself, he had been speaking prose all of his life.

So I have tried to think about the ways in which nature writing constitutes a tradition and about my relation to it. I will begin by saying that, patronymic circumstances notwithstanding, the relation is not familial. John Burroughs is no distant kinsman of mine, although it would please a lot of my cousins to claim him if they could, at the same time, disclaim me. But the relation is familial in an unapparent way: forty-five years ago, John Hay won this award. He is New England born and bred and has the great, complex legacy of Emerson, Thoreau, and John Burroughs as a liberating part of his living and breathing. He has been, all of his life and in all of his work, every inch a nature writer, and now stands as an indispensable part of a tradition that has been indispensably part of him. He is also my father-in-law. In that capacity, we have known and born each other good will for more than forty years, but remain, figuratively speaking, inhabitants of distant lands—places that we read about, but could not write about to save our souls.

The following reflections are improvised, as simple and sincere as I can make them, but less than ideally clear. Like the Moliere character, I'm still getting the hang of speaking in prose.

We all know, because we have all been told, that the idea of wilderness lies behind many conceptions and expressions of Americanness, and therefore of American Nature and American Nature Writing. Ideas have their own publicity apparatus and spokespersons. Facts have to manage on their own. The fact is, that for the great majority of American nature writers, American poets and novelists, and Americans in general, the primeval landscape has always been an uninhabitable Elsewhere, like the horizon. The *de facto* landscape that has enabled us to think of ourselves as Nature's Nation has been the local outback. As the wilderness retreated before the axe, the plow, the bulldozer, and the venturesome capitalist, another kind of nature slipped into the spaces it left behind. Thoreau was very well aware that the woodlot he squatted on at Walden Pond had had former inhabitants; it was wilder in his time than it had been in theirs. After his death, it would become wilder yet, reoccupied by creatures he associated with the wilderness to the north and west of him: deer, turkey, beaver, coyote. The same is true of the place where John Burroughs, emulating Thoreau, built his secluded cabin,

Slabsides, on a hilly, nine-acre woodlot on the Hudson River. Euro-Americans had occupied this area for more than two centuries at the time of his birth — it wasn't any closer to wilderness and the forest primeval than Manhattan Island. John Hay spent the happiest days of his boyhood on Lake Sunapee, in southern New Hampshire, in a region that had been settled and cleared since before the American Revolution. Aldo Leopold's Sand County, where he built a cabin and became an ecologist, was farther west and in newer country, but it was still a long way from wilderness.

The experience of the local outback is more often one of intimacy than of sublimity, and it is routinely an encounter with local history. A church or bank in town, or a warehouse along an urban waterfront, may in fact be a lot older than the cellar hole, stone wall, feldspar quarry, or narrow gauge logging railway you come across in the woods, but it does not have the same power to make you consider yourself in the light of history, or to think about how history and nature are, in the last analysis, bedfellows. This truth jumps out at you when you look at old photographs of your local outback. They are apt to show a landscape as treeless as the west of Ireland. It is less obvious, but no less true, when you look at a contemporary photograph of the same place, all reverted to woodland now. It resembles nothing that has been seen for centuries in the west of Ireland or most other places in the developed world. It is distinctively American.

I hope I do not overestimate the influence of this kind of landscape on American writers. I cannot overestimate its influence on this one, both to my growing up and now, in my old age. Over the course of my life, it has assumed a figurative significance, in no way at the expense of its very downright and literal one. The local outback — the cutover swamps across the street from the South Carolina house I grew up in; the scruffy woodlot that is more or less my backyard in Maine — fostered and sustained those vagrant, truant tendencies that it is the proper business of formal education to domesticate, discipline, cultivate, and make productive. In the process of fostering them, it also becomes analogous to them. It is an indication of the thoroughness of my education that I became an educator myself. It is indicative of its incompleteness — its unclaimed outback — that I eventually became a writer, or at least became the particular kind of writer that I am.

I will venture the same generalization about the tradition of nature writing. It is not only that it has often had its origins in local outbacks; it too exists as a kind of analogy to them. Beginning with Thoreau, it grew up quietly, largely overlooked. It slowly emerged as a new feature of the literary landscape, which is to say a new habitat for the imagination, one that can be experienced in a library. One day, perhaps, such local outbacks, like the frontier itself, will be experienced only there. But not yet; not on our watch.

In quietly fostering and sustaining this kind of writing, the John Burroughs Association has been six or seven decades ahead of American English Departments, which have only recently deigned to claim it as a proper academic field. More importantly, the Association has, through its choices, constantly reviewed, enriched, and updated our idea of what this kind of writing is, where it has been, and where it may be headed.

Writers or not, we cannot always choose our company. Sometimes, it chooses us. I could not be more honored by the choice. Thank you so much.

Deep South

I was invited to write this essay for National Geographic *magazine. It was published in the November 2014 edition.*

Audubon's Long-billed Curlews — two majestic and improbable birds — hung over the mantle in my parents' house. Behind them lies Charleston Harbor, with one of its famous forts in the middle distance and the city itself in the far background. In South Carolina, history and natural history cohabited. The oldest places I knew were the wildest places I knew: the antebellum rice-field country and the barrier islands, which began twenty miles south of Conway, where we lived, and stretched from there, past Georgetown and Charleston and on to the Georgia line.

History had populated those places, then depopulated them. Their teeming life — fish, flesh, and fowl, to say nothing of snakes, sea turtles, and alligators — and their sense of vanished human presence gave rise to two rumors. One was that cougars still lurked in the deepest swamps. The other was that ghosts hung around particular plantations. Reliable people saw unaccountable things. That is what other reliable people told you, and what you secretly wished to believe.

I left South Carolina for good more than sixty years ago.

Since then, history has repopulated much of that old country. There is a new prosperity, a new and glittering worldliness. Before I left, I'd heard about Kiawah Island and dreamed of getting there — a big, history-haunted place, its sea-island cotton plantations long gone. As a boy, it sounded to me like a sort of paradise — miles of empty beach on one side, miles of salt marsh and tidal creek on the other, separated by a virtual jungle of second growth maritime forest.

Kiawah has now become somebody else's idea of paradise: 3,000 housing units, a luxury hotel, an international clientele, and a new identity, based on upscale residential development and tourism. What happened there has happened and is still happening all along the Southeastern coast, to places I once imagined to be like churches or famous battlefields, protected by their history from history itself.

Last spring, I actually saw Kiawah for the first time. I chartered a plane to fly me from just north of Charleston down to the ACE (Ashepoo, Combahee, Edisto) Basin, twenty miles south of the city. We passed over the harbor — Fort Sumter, ugly as a wart, just below us; to the west, the skyline of the old city, much the same as it had been in 1831, when Audubon had painted his curlews — and soon had Kiawah in sight. The pilot gestured toward a golf course at the north end.

"They had the Ryder Cup there in 1991. I watched some of it and got to look around Kiawah. Man, that place is paradise, if you're rich enough. Wish I was."

The golf course, the nicely landscaped neighborhoods of the interior, and the long wide beach were truly beautiful, lying quietly in the soft light of a spring morning. No hope of seeing a cougar there, but Tiger Woods was a possibility, I supposed. That was a different fantasy of paradise. I felt pre-empted and disenfranchised by it.

Only a few miles south of Kiawah, St. Helena Sound makes a deep indentation in the coast. Otter Island — smaller than Kiawah, but not small — guards its northeastern edge. I stared down, made up my mind to get there ASAP. Then we crossed over the sound on a southwesterly bearing, and followed the Combahee River inland, to the little crossroads town of Yemassee, where the river unravels into small, parallel channels, assumes the name of Salkehatchie, and loses itself in the swamps. At Yemassee, we angled back to the north, crossing the headwaters of the Ashepoo and reaching the last, and largest, of the eponymous rivers, the Edisto. We followed it back to the coast, completing a perfunctory and preliminary circuit of the ACE Basin.

The history of rice cultivation was written on the landscape — along the rivers, dikes enclosed fields, which were subdivided by drainage ditches that fed into larger canals. The system depended on tidal fresh water; it had worked only in the narrow region that was far enough upriver to be beyond the reach of salt water, but far enough downriver to have significant tides. *Trunks*, ingenious double-gated spillways, could arrest the tides, keeping the fields dry for plowing and planting, flooding them to precisely regulated levels as the rice grew, and draining them again for harvest in the fall. On this March day, most of the fields were drained, and tractors were at work on several. Corn, I would learn, was the primary crop. The fields would remain dry all summer, and be flooded in the fall, with the unharvested corn still standing. Ducks would harvest the corn; hunters would harvest the ducks.

I saw only two-laned roads, many of them unpaved, and visible only when they emerged from the canopy of the woods to cross marshes or rivers on causeways or bridges. The region was in fact an archipelago of low islands, separated and veined by a maze of winding creeks, rivers, marshlands, and swamps. A few modest houses were scattered along the roads, and there was a dock, with a couple of trawlers tied up to it, and a public boat launch near the mouth of the Ashepoo. Nothing looked like the South Carolina of the 21st century; indeed, it looked more like the South Carolina I had heard my father describe than the one I had rummaged around in fifty years ago.

This landscape took shape well before the American Revolution. The bloody Yemassee War of 1715 had left the planters firmly in control of the region. Their earliest method of rice planting involved the damming of narrow swamps, and using the impoundments thus created (called *reserves* in South Carolina) to flood the fields below them at the appropriate time. The trunk and dike system allowed cultivation on a much larger scale and generated great wealth for many of the planters. Even by South Carolina standards, these planters were ardently secessionist, and they paid for it in the Civil War. Federal troops quickly gained control of several barrier islands. The planters lit out for the interior, leaving their plantations to be burned, and their slaves to be emancipated, by Federal gunboats and raiding parties.

After the War, an ACE basin planter returned to find what he described as a "howling wilderness" — the dikes broken down, the ditches clogged and overgrown. Cordgrass, cattails, needle rush, and bulrush completed the conversion of tillage land into marsh. Wildlife flourished in these disimproved places, and wealthy sportsmen, many of them Yankees, bought up the old plantations. To the extent that they maintained the rice fields and the uplands, these new owners did so for the sake of deer, quail, turkey, dove, and especially ducks. They spent their winters pursuing those creatures, living sometimes in plantation houses that had managed to survive the war, sometimes in houses they themselves built, often on the site of the original house.

Decades passed; the new prosperity established itself; waterfront property grew ever scarcer and ever more valuable. A little way to the north, strip malls, housing developments, and upscale Elysiums like Kiawah stretched southward from Charleston (giving it, according to a survey done in 2007, the worst commuter traffic of any midsized metropolis in the nation); a little to the south, the old town of Beaufort sprawled northward. The ACE, as a functioning historical landscape and a relatively intact and exceptionally rich ecosystem, grew ever more anachronistic economically and ever more indispensable biologically.

The effort to protect it began two decades ago. Crucial habitats were identified; their owners were approached. An alphabet soup of agencies, foundations, and non-profit organizations — some national, some local — was enlisted: U.S. Fish and Wildlife (USFW); National Estuarine Research Reserve (NERR); South Carolina Department of Natural Resources (SCDNR); The Nature Conservancy (TNR); Ducks Unlimited (DU); the Nemours Wildlife Foundation (NWF): the Lowcountry Open Land Trust (LOLT) — the list goes on. John Frampton, of SCDNR, served as the coordinator. He described the process for me:

"If we went down there from Columbia with a master plan, we'd have been dead on arrival. So our plan was just to keep the ACE Basin exactly the way it was the day we started. We had a lot of cooks in the kitchen. We agreed to co-operate where we could, not to go public when we couldn't, or fight over who got credit for what. It took a lot of meetings, a lot of time and patience — we listened more than we talked and relied on one-on-

one conversations and word-of-mouth conversions. Local people know who to approach and who should approach them. That was key."

The work is ongoing. The ACE Basin, as currently delineated, consists of roughly 350,000 acres of upland, marsh, diked fields, and coastal islands. Approximately half of this acreage is protected — some of it having been sold or donated to public agencies, like SCDNR, USFW, NERR, and some remaining private, but with conservation or stewardship easements that preclude subdivision and development.

That is all background. I have now spent enough time in the foreground, driving, walking, canoeing and boating in the ACE to know that it would take several well-spent lifetimes to speak of it with any authority, and several books to describe its history, its natural history, and their complicated co-evolution. I walked on Otter Island, one of the gems, but only one of the ACE. Dean Harrigal, who oversaw the ACE for SCDNR, had taken me there. He spoke of the Civil War fortifications that lay somewhere in the dense growth of the interior: a battery established by the Confederates in 1861, seized by Federal forces in the same year, and turned into a signal station. A colony of self-emancipated slaves grew up around it. No sign of these things, or of any other human enterprise, remained. We did not happen to see any long-billed curlews, but we did see whimbrels, godwits, willets, oystercatchers, red knots, dunlins, and plovers. Their cries, the thumping and sighing of the surf, the rattling of the wind in the palmettos, and the squeak of sand underfoot were the only sounds. The place could have been waiting for Robinson Crusoe to stagger ashore and its history to begin.

Dean's constituents include the hunters, fishermen, and bird watchers who avail themselves of two state-owned Game Management Areas (GMAs) — one, at Bear Island, is predominantly restored rice field; the other, Donnelley, is primarily upland, although it includes several hundred acres of old rice field and a beautiful reserve. His constituents are also landowners and representatives of all the agencies who have played a role or might play a role in keeping the ACE the way it was. He talks to students, some in local elementary schools, and some in graduate programs; he enlists the interest, support, and energy of local community leaders. The job requires tact, polite persistence, affability, and a lot of initiative and responsibility, and he appeared to me to have those qualities abundantly. But his other constituents were critters — game species, to be sure, but also those shorebirds out on Otter, or the wood storks, herons, anhingas, egrets, and ibis that nest at the upper end of the reserve that lies out behind his office, on the Donnelly GMA. He keeps an eye on comparatively endangered species, like the swallow-tailed kite, salt marsh mink, loggerhead turtle, and Eastern diamondback rattlesnake, but also on the invertebrates that multiply prodigiously in the warm, shallow water of a partially flooded field, and are crucial to particular migratory birds at particular seasons. His knowledge, curiosity, and attentiveness made him the finest kind of guide to the ACE, and I abused his hospitality at every opportunity.

He showed me places I would never have found and things I would never have noticed: back in the woods, on a slight knoll overlooking the Cheehaw River, a tributary of the Combahee, were several low burial vaults under an ancient, collapsing live oak. The surrounding trees were big and widely spaced — a magnolia, a beech, a holly, a walnut. "Those trees were planted," he said. "You don't find them growing in the same spot like that naturally. Somebody wanted this to be like an arboretum. And that little ditch along the edge of the marsh? I think it was a small canal, big enough to float the crops down to the river. There was a whole life here." Further down the Cheehaw, another vault, quite a fine one, dating from before the Revolution, stood in front of the overgrown earthworks of a Confederate battery, built to protect a bridge on the Charleston-Savannah railway, a little further upriver. Behind the earthworks, scattered in low woods, were the tombstones of slaves, former slaves, and their descendants; a spare cinderblock church, still in use, was half a mile away. "Whenever we sign an easement or a property transfer," Dean said, "I tell people that with one stroke of the pen we're preserving our heritage and our environment. It's a good line. And it's the truth."

You can stand on one of the dikes in the Bear Island Refuge and imagine that a chunk of Holland had been set down in the New World. There are no cities or windmills, and not many people; but there is a greater variety, abundance, and obviousness of animal life than I have seen anywhere else in North America. In one canal beside a dike, I counted over a hundred alligators, most of them still as stumps. Black skimmers, flying low and straight, their lower mandibles shearing the water, lifted over their motionless heads as casually as a man stepping over a log. About five hundred storks, ibis, egrets, and white pelicans stood along the bank, as though waiting for a parade to start.

It has now been several years since *National Geographic* sent me to the ACE Basin. Since then, I've managed to get back a few times. But my great, emblematic memory of the ACE Basin comes from my first trip. Dean was driving past a small, mostly drained former rice field in the Donnelly WMA. He eased the truck to a stop and handed me his binoculars. "Look out there and tell me what you see." I glanced, and saw the usual suspects — herons, a glossy ibis, and, oddly, an immature eagle, standing on the mud. On either side of it were two big white birds. They walked with a stoop but weren't storks. Or egrets. Or ibis. I raised the binoculars and stared, then handed them back to Dean and said I did not believe it. A pair of whooping cranes.

When I was a boy, there were said to be twenty-nine of them on earth. Now there are a few hundred. Until three years ago, when this pair appeared, the last time one had been seen in South Carolina was 1850. "This summer, they'll be old enough to breed. If three come back next fall, it could be the beginning of something." As it turned out, the cranes returned for a few years, but never became a breeding pair. But seeing them in this place suggested natural possibilities that seem almost supernatural.

But Dean is adamant about one of those possibilities, and so was every other wildlife biologist I met down there: "I don't care what you hear or who you hear it from," he said. "There are NO COUGARS in the ACE Basin. Elvis? Maybe. UFOs? I wouldn't rule it out. But cougars? No. No way."

So, sure enough, back home in the deep north, I'm chatting with a friend. He's originally from Charleston, knows the ACE Basin. He's a reliable, skeptical fellow, and a wildlife biologist himself.

It wasn't him. It was his cousin, whom he'd vouch for, even though it happened late at night, and the cousin was tired. He was slowly driving down an oak-lined avenue that led in to one of the plantations where he was visiting. The thing materialized out of the woods, loped down the road ahead of him, in no great hurry. He knew what bobcats look like. Also, what dogs, foxes, and coyotes look like. This animal was big, very long tailed, and about the color and consistency of smoke. It turned, eyes glittering in the headlights, then bounded into the shadows.

The evidence of one kind of faith is the evidence of things not seen, or half-seen.

The evidence of another kind of faith is fact: the ACE Basin itself.

The Deep North

In 2003, I wrote a brief essay, entitled "Borealis," for an anthology called On Wilderness: Voices from Maine. *Its focus was primarily on Maine's North Woods, not on my first experience with the Deep North, which had been in the summer of 1963, in Northern Quebec.*

I have changed the title to "The Deep North," and greatly expanded the original essay. It now deals in much greater detail with my Canadian summer, which has informed the whole of my adult life.

GETTING THERE

I grew up in the South. There, the Deep North was one of the legendary geographies of childhood, like the Wild West, Darkest Africa, or the India of Kipling's *Just So* stories. The first rumors of the Deep North reached me through picture-book stories about Paul Bunyan and Babe the Blue Ox and a weekly radio program about Sergeant Preston of the Yukon ("On King! On you huskies!"); later I read the stories of Russell Annabel in *Sports Afield*; and the novels of writers like James Oliver Curwood (*Nomads of the North*) and Jack London (*Call of the Wild, White Fang*). Legendary geography nurtures the sense of magical possibility, a homeland for the imagination. Children crave it; tourism sells it; religions offer many varieties of it. I relocated from the South to Maine, the homeland of Paul

Bunyan, in 1968, and am still here. Maine has done about all that actual geography can do, fulfilling and annihilating daydreams about living otherwise or elsewhere.

But Maine was not my first or deepest encounter with the Deep North. That occurred in 1963, at a place called Cooper Lake, about two hundred miles north of La Tuque, in the Province of Quebec. I got a job there through dumb luck — on spring vacation during my junior year of college, a friend of my father's had asked me about my plans for the summer. I told him I hoped to find a job Montreal or Quebec City, in order to improve my French, which was mostly bookish, and had been only slightly ameliorated by my having spent the previous summer in France. The man, who was in the timber business, knew somebody who might be able to help. By mid-June, I was in northern Quebec working as a compass man — a timber cruiser's assistant — for the Canadian International Paper Company. CIP had a huge leasehold in the province; the town of La Tuque was at its southern edge.

I flew to Montreal at the end of May, and next morning took a bus to Three Rivers, which is on the St. Lawrence River, about halfway between Montreal and Quebec City. You may be as surprised as I was to learn that Three Rivers is the second-oldest municipality in Canada — only Quebec City itself is older.

It was cold and drizzly when we left Montreal. My cold-weather clothes, such as they were, were in my duffle bag, in the bus's baggage compartment, but the bus itself was warm, quiet, uncrowded, and comfortable. I read, occasionally dozing off. Three Rivers turned out to be a mid-sized mill city. The town itself no more suggested the Deep North than Cairo, Illinois, suggests the Wild West or the Deep South, although two hundred years ago its position, at the confluence of the Ohio and the Mississippi, had made it the gateway to both. But soon after I changed buses in Three Rivers, and headed toward La Tuque, things began looking up. The road ran northward up the valley of the St. Maurice River and gave us occasional views of it. It was a whitewater river, and with the spring runoff still in progress, it was impressively wild. I had only the dimmest notion of whitewater canoeing and log drives, but this was beginning to look like the Deep North sure enough.

About halfway between Three Rivers and La Tuque, our driver pulled the bus over onto an unpaved lay-by — a couple of outhouses, a few picnic tables, and a handsome view down to the river. The rain had stopped, but the day remained raw and chilly. We did not linger. There were more of us than I would have expected, considering that we were going to a small town at the dead end of a winding road that had very little traffic on it. It would have seemed natural to strike up a conversation — to ask people about La Tuque, and their own reasons for going there. But I was in Canada, where people are not nosy, self-important, garrulous, or overly familiar, as Americans in general tend to be. Or at least that is how Americans in the South, the only ones I'd had much contact with, tended to be. And, truth be told, how I often tend to be myself.

The weather was clearing by the time we pulled into La Tuque. It was a grim-looking little place, a paper-mill town. On the outskirts, residential streets ran perpendicular to the highway, houses along both sides of them. There were no sidewalks, and the houses were set close together, three or four stories high, flat roofed, and cheaply built. They were designed for one very large family or two or three smaller ones. The upper floors had small porches, and on several of them, clotheslines mounted on pulleys ran across a narrow alleyway to the house opposite.

The small downtown — streets, shops, and sidewalks — was only two or three blocks wide. We passed a big hotel, four stories high, flat-roofed, and about half a block long. Its double doors, in the center of the building, opened directly onto the sidewalk. A big sign mounted on the roof and pointing down toward the front door announced that this was the Windsor Hotel. Why such a big hotel in such an unprepossessing town?

At the bus station, the driver got down, opened the luggage compartment, and began pulling out suitcases, trunks, and eventually my duffle bag. He asked where I was headed. His English was perfectly intelligible, but with a French inflection. *"Lac Cooper,"* I said, more or less in French: Lak Coo-*PER*.

"Ah. Coop'lak. They tell you inside where t'catch th' bush bus."

Inside, the station was crowded, but somebody immediately came up to me — would I be Franklin Burroughs? He'd probably noticed the *Lt. F. Burroughs, US NAVY* stenciled on my duffle bag. In 1945, Daddy brought his gear home from the Pacific in it. He passed it on to me when I went off to college. But that occurred to me only later. Being picked out of the crowd like that had made me feel as though I had *Greenhorn* or *Imposter* written in red letters on my forehead — a sensation by no means unfamiliar to me.

The man introduced himself as Andrew Stevens. He told me that I wouldn't be going to Cooper Lake immediately. There was a big forest fire up around James Bay, and most of the timber cruisers were there, helping with the firefighting. They'd get back to Cooper Lake — as he called it — in a week or two. In the meanwhile, he was going to drive me up to Lac de La Grosse Ile — French pronunciation this time — where CIP had a fishing camp. But first we should get lunch, over at the Windsor Hotel. We went out to the parking lot, threw my duffle bag onto the back seat of a drab and dented VW Beetle, and walked over to the hotel.

The dining room was fancier than you'd expect: place settings with bright stainless-steel utensils, cloth napkins, cloth placemats; a hostess to hand you a menu and lead you over to your table; a waiter, wearing a dark coat, appearing immediately to take your order, make recommendations, suggest a wine. I don't remember what we ordered or how it tasted, only the incongruity of such a restaurant in such a place.

After the meal we got into the VW and drove a block or two north, where the street and the paved road ended and there was a gate. An attendant waved us through. We were well away from the St. Maurice River by now — it lay somewhere off to our west. The road we traveled was as big as an ordinary two-laned highway, but it was rough. Its posted speed limit — 25 MPH — was basically self-re-enforcing, and might as well have read *Do Your Damnedest*. The VW banged and jolted along. Andrew said it was a company car — CIP preferred VWs to pickups or jeeps. They were cheaper to buy, cheaper to operate, rugged, and their short wheelbase gave them good road clearance. All of them carried in the front luggage compartment a come-along, a length of heavy rope, an axe, first-aid kit, sleeping bag, matches, canned goods, and a few candy bars. The roads were often slippery with mud, ice, or snow, depending on the season of the year, but VWs were so light that you could usually get yourself out of a ditch or snowbank with the come-along, perhaps using a spruce sapling for a pry bar, and be on your way.

Andrew was only a few years older than me, a law student from Ottawa. His job with CIP was a summer internship. He worked out of the home office in Montreal. He'd been sent up to La Tuque because there'd been a fatality in one of the camps — a *bucheron* had been killed by a falling tree. In all cases involving fatalities, CIP sent an intern up to get details, depose witnesses, visit and photograph the accident site. Andrew had planned to leave early this morning — it was a long drive up to this particular camp — but the home office called him last night and told him to wait until I arrived, drive me to Lac de la Grosse Ile in the afternoon, and stay the night there. A float plane from where the accident had occurred would pick him up first thing tomorrow morning. He was happy to do it. He told me how much he enjoyed flying in a small plane up here. There was no other way to appreciate the extent of Canada's north country — how empty it was, how endless it was, and how much water it had. The float plane from the logging camp would have him to the lake nearest to the scene of the accident by midmorning. A CIP representative would meet him there, drive him to the site, provide him with all the information pertaining to the dead man's employment history, his next of kin, dependents, and so forth. He didn't expect any complications — logging was a dangerous business, so accidents like this one had plenty of precedents, and almost always were settled out of court. He could get back to Lac de la Grosse Ile in time for an early supper and drive on back to La Tuque immediately afterwards.

I asked him about the fishing camp. He told me that CIP had built it for their upper management — not for the likes of him. Most of them scheduled their visits later in the summer, after the weather and the water had warmed up, and the black flies had quieted down. The camp had a nice beach, a fine place for swimming, and there was the lake itself for canoeing, motorboating, picnicking. Fine place for kids too. The fishing was still good even then, but it was at its very best now, just after ice-out. This was the time of year the sports — the serious fishermen — liked to come up. The camp had seven guides — Cree Indians — a cook, and a cook boy. I would bunk with the cook boy and the guides and eat my meals with them.

The camp had been built mainly by Emile Richard, who now ran it. He would have plenty of use for an extra hand. He liked to keep things ship-shape, and between repairing winter damage, tidying and tightening things up, seeing to the needs of the sports, keeping the books and ordering supplies, he had a lot to do. And there was always firewood to buck up, split, and stack for next year. Woodstoves were used for all of the heating and cooking.

Andrew said the food at the camp would be a cut above the usual North Woods fare. A lot of it was flown in fresh from Montreal or Quebec City. The guides and I would eat earlier than the sports, who liked to clean up after a day of fishing and perhaps have a drink or two before supper. Andrew would eat with them. He thought it likely that he'd have wine with his meal, and unlikely that I would with mine.

Late in the afternoon, we turned off the main IP road and onto something that was like a long private driveway. It was not deeply rutted and was muddy only in a few low spots. Grass edged out from the shoulders and grew along the center hump. We had just crossed over a fair-sized stream when I saw, sitting in the middle of the road and plain as day, a snowshoe hare. It was splotchy tan and white above, with long hind legs and white, ridiculously oversized hind feet. It hippity-hopped along ahead of us, then swerved out of the middle of the road and into the weeds along the shoulder. There it crouched, ears laid back along its shoulders and pink nose twitching. If I'd been alone, I would have stopped and stared, because a snowshoe rabbit, like a porcupine, an ermine, a moose, or a beaver was a half-mythical creature. I'd read accounts and seen illustrations of them. They belonged to the legendary fauna of the Deep North. The behavior of this one was prosaic — dim-witted and timorous. It couldn't decide whether sitting tight or high tailing it was the best survival strategy. I remarked to Andrew that this was the first time I'd actually seen a snowshoe hare. He said that this was an awkward, in-between season for them. There was still snow on the ground in low places and under young spruce trees, but out in the open now they stood out like a sore thumb. In another few weeks, they'd be brown all over.

We got to the fishing camp in the shank of the afternoon. The guides and their sports were still out on the water. I stowed my duffle bag in the bunkroom and went out to look around. I was here, in the taiga of Northern Quebec, a place essentially unchanged since the end of the last Ice Age, which is to say, since human history first began to emerge and differentiate itself from natural history in this part of the world — the point where myth begins.

When Andrew had driven us out through the gate at the end of the paved road in La Tuque, we were in fact entering two enormous ecosystems, one natural and the other human. I will take them one at a time.

The Woods of Quebec, North of La Tuque

I had derived my haphazard conception of the Deep North from books and magazine articles that were, in fact, mostly about Alaska. My conception of the Deep North's Wild East boiled down to Paul Bunyan and Babe the Blue Ox. And to the extent that my mental image of the Deep North, east or west, involved forests, I imagined it to consist of enormous trees, most of them conifers. They would be enormous because they had never been cut. It stood to reason.

I knew that if you went far enough northward, you passed the tree line and entered the treeless tundra, but I never thought at all about what happened to the boreal forest as it approached its northern extremity.

When Susan and I moved to Maine five years later, it took us no time at all to learn that people still spoke of its northern half as a place apart. Within another five years, I'd taken to going to different parts of Maine's Deep North for purposes of canoeing and fishing. There were not many towns up there, and not many paved roads. Most of the land consisted of townships. Some of these had names — King and Bartlett township, Attean township, etc. Others were designated only by a combination of letters and numbers which located them on a grid — e.g. T5 R7 BKP WKR. The townships amount to a kind of arrested frontier. Going all the way back to colonial times, they have been owned by absentee landlords. For the past couple of centuries, most of these landlords have been in the timber and/or pulp and paper business. In all, they cover an area the size of Massachusetts. In theory, they are still waiting for homesteaders to come and form enough of a community to be classified as a *plantation*, with its own post office and limited powers of self-governance, and then, with sufficient growth in population, to be chartered as a town. That can take a while. The Forks Plantation, in northwestern Somerset County, is at present 164 years old.

Throughout their long history, the unorganized territories have been logged again and again. Speaking very broadly, the progression has been from pine lumber to spruce lumber to pulpwood. Early Euro-Americans prized white pine particularly for shipbuilding — its size, comparatively light weight, straight grain, and flexibility made it ideal for masts and spars. It was also an easy wood to work — to plane, sand, shape, and carve. Houses were framed, sheathed, floored, and roofed with it; all manner of furniture, plain and fancy, was made from it. As early as 1853, lumbermen were telling Thoreau that the best of the white pines — those famous ones upon whose stumps a yoke of oxen could stand — had long since disappeared, and lumberjacks now gladly took trees they would not have looked at twice a decade earlier. Spruce and fir gradually replaced white pine. The best specimens were not as splendid as the even moderately good white pines, nor was their lumber as versatile, but fine spruce was abundant and often handy to water, and provided good quality lumber, particularly as timbers for framing and planks for roofing and siding. Pulpwood — the primary product of Maine's north woods now — can use almost any conifer, plus aspen; the quality of the individual tree — whether tall and straight or stunted and twisted — does not matter. If one relies solely on natural regeneration, it takes about a biblically-defined human lifespan — threescore and ten years — for a clearcut stand to grow into pulpwood of harvestable size.

Not since the days of axes, crosscut saws, teams of oxen and draft horses, and river-drivers with their peavies, pikes, and caulked boots has the commercial harvesting of trees been picturesque in itself and relatively benign in its effects on the landscape. In the twenty-first century, I doubt that any method of harvesting wood in North America exceeds in its environmental destructiveness a contemporary pulpwood operation. Neil Rolde opens his fine book, *The Interrupted Forest*, with the description of a logging operation in Hancock County in September of 1998. It requires only two men — three if you count the driver of the truck that takes the logs from the woods to the mill. One of these men is in the cab of a "monstrous mobile instrument" called a feller-buncher, mounted on caterpillar treads like an army tank. It has hydraulic shears on its front end, with iron bars above them, which are used to grip the standing tree and hold it up-right. The shears cut the tree, leaving only a low stump. The feller-buncher backs up, removing that tree from the forest and laying it flat. The other enormous machine slices the branches away from each prostrate tree, cuts it into logs of the desired length, and piles them in bunches, where the big tractor-trailer truck can pick them up and deliver them to the nearest mill. What is left at the end of one of these operations is a clearcut. Rolde describes its muddy, torn, and gutted earth as looking like the no man's land between French and German lines at Verdun, circa 1917.

The obvious analogy to this sort of highly mechanized, capitalized, and efficient forestry is American agribusiness. In-creasingly gigantic tractors that combine the functions of reap-ing, threshing, and winnowing allow one operator to harvest and load more grain from more acres in a day than a dozen small independent farmers could have managed fifty years ago. Cumulatively, all farming depletes the soil — "a gentler form of mining" as an old friend calls it. Chemical fertilizers maintain its productivity, but they do not replenish the accumulated humus of what had once been tallgrass prairies of the Midwest, or the deep delta soils of California's central valley or the lower Mississippi Basin. The end result is industrial monoculture. Its benefits are undeniable — food costs accounted for about 40% of a household budget in 1900, and about 10% of it at present. But the environmental costs are compounding and cumulative: floods, droughts, wind erosion, dire reduction of anadromous and oceanic fisheries.

Since the publication of *The Interrupted Forest,* the harvest-ing of pulpwood has achieved an even greater efficiency through widespread use of the whole tree chipper. Felled trees can be fed directly into it, branches and all, and the chipped wood blown into a big tractor trailer truck. A middleman — the operator of the machine that removed the limbs from felled trees and cut them into logs, which then had to be loaded onto tractor trailer trucks — is thus eliminated. No unsightly and obstructive slash — limbs and treetops — remains behind. This simplifies and expedites replanting the clearcut with seedlings of particularly desirable — disease-resistant and fast-growing — species. Of course, the unsightly and obstructive slash was also biomass; its removal further impoverishes the soil and accelerates erosion from rainfall and the spring thaw.

Knocking around in the unorganized territories means driving on private, unpaved roads. When I first began going up there, most of these roads were single-lane affairs; the roadside trees arched over them. The typical logging operation involved a small crew — men with chain saws, a skidder and its operator, and a flatbed truck and its driver. The cutting was selective — perhaps by species, perhaps by the size of the tree. There were no big clearcuts, no driving for miles past the World War I landscape Rolde describes, or past the newer, even more denuded ones made possible by the whole tree chippers.

The land we drove over, even then, almost invariably belonged to paper companies. But they clearly were continuing to harvest trees for other purposes as well, and sometimes I would see a truck laden exclusively with big yellow birch logs — probably Maine's most versatile high-quality hardwood — or with hemlock, cedar, pine, white ash, or white birch, all of a size indicating that they had been cut for lumber, not for pulp.

We learn and know by analogy. The Canadian Wilderness provided my closest analogy to the unorganized territories of Maine. Both were the land of the snowshoe hare, the beaver, the moose, the loon, the blackfly, the canoe, the whitewater river, and many, many lakes, ponds, bogs and streams. Northern Quebec was of course far wilder, far more extensive, and far more remote than even the remotest corners of Maine's Deep North. But in Maine I began to realize, for the first time, that Canada north of La Tuque, which I had seen in 1963, had never been the natural habitat of Paul Bunyan. No towering white pines grew there. The rich valley of the great Gulf of Saint Lawrence formed the northerly limit for them and for many trees, both coniferous and deciduous, that were common in Maine. These included most of our biggest species — hemlock, for example, and many of our prized hardwoods, like yellow birch and even sugar maple, the emblem of Canada. The impression I had had on the way to La Tuque, that as the bus made its way northward from Three Rivers along the Saint Maurice River, we were entering a wilder, wider country, was correct. It was also a country with fewer species of trees, and those trees — primarily spruce, fir, cedar, aspen, and birch — did not reach the size that they did in Maine. What I mostly found there was something that would be a contradiction in terms in Maine: old growth pulpwood.

CIP. The Artificial Ecosystem

The Deep North of literature and legend was a land of enormous silences and solitude. In fiction, the protagonists travel alone or in a small group, generally by dog sled or on snowshoes. Their survival depends upon their resolution and resourcefulness. I, on the other hand, was a low-level, semi-skilled corporate employee. The boreal wilderness through which I travelled was administered by the Canadian government and leased by CIP. Insofar as my basic needs — food, shelter, transportation, human companionship, mail service, and a paycheck — were concerned, CIP provided them.

I did not know much about CIP when I went to Canada, and I learned about it only in the most haphazard, unsystematic way. I knew that it leased an enormous swath of territory in Quebec and the maritime provinces; I assumed, correctly, that it was an offshoot of the American corporation that was simply called International Paper — IP. IP owned a paper mill in Georgetown, South Carolina. At one time, it had been the largest paper mill in the world. Georgetown was forty miles south of Conway, where I grew up; when the wind was from that direction, we could smell it. People called it the smell of money — a sulfurous, rotten-egg stink. By analogy, I assumed that the paper mills I had seen in Three Rivers and La Tuque belonged to CIP. That assumption was also correct.

The men who felled the pulp that fed the big mill in Georgetown were independent contractors, paid by the cord, and not employees of IP itself. Often these contractors were themselves corporations, owning some large woodland properties and purchasing the timber rights on others. My father's friend, to whom I had spoken about wanting a summer job in Montreal or Quebec, was the head of one such corporation.

In 1963, I was an undergraduate English major with no curiosity about corporations and how they worked, or about the differences between Canadian and American corporations in general or between IP and CIP in particular. My only qualification for being a compass man for CIP was that I had for a couple of summers worked as a compass man in South Carolina. There it was a simple job — most of it could have been performed by an intelligent dog, if the dog had been able to use a tape measure and a paint gun.

I did not keep any sort of journal while I was in Quebec. When I was cleaning out my parents' house, after Mama died in 2008 (Daddy had died twelve years earlier), I found a mass of old letters in a plastic garbage bag in the attic. These included all the letters I had written to them since I went off to college in 1960. Bundled together and wrapped in string were a dozen or so from Canada. The longest and most useful describe my two-week stint at Lac de La Grosse Isle, where I was staying in one place and had time enough to write. All of my letters from Canada are what letters between parents and children tend to be — merely newsy and reassuring. But they bring back memories that had grown indistinct. That is particularly true of my one letter from Lac de La Grosse Ile, a place I had almost forgotten about.

Lac de La Grosse Isle was not the most exciting part of my summer. I saw far more of the Canadian wilderness when I got to Cooper Lake. But Lac de La Grosse Ile did provide my first, and most comprehensive, introduction to the whole range of CIP's personnel, from the various executives back in Montreal, who were entitled to spend three or four days at Lac de La Grosse Isle as a normal perk, down to the Cree guides, who were merely seasonal employees. I had the impression that the guides spent the off-season trapping, hunting and fishing as they had always done — to bring in some income, and to feed themselves, their families, and their remoter kin. Maurice the cook boy and I would have been more or less equivalent to them hierarchically, in that we were also seasonal employees. Maurice would return to La Tuque for his senior year of high school at the end of the summer, and I would return to Sewanee for my final year of college. Maurice had started working for CIP two summers earlier, beginning what amounted to an apprenticeship: he was learning how to become a CIP cook. To that extent, the company had an investment in him. They had no such investment in me. I was working for CIP only because strings had been pulled to in South Carolina.

The cook, Gilbert, was well into his fifties, and so he was a relatively senior figure. He had probably started off like Maurice, as a cook boy. Perhaps he had been transferred from one of the ordinary logging camps to this camp because he was an unusually good cook, or perhaps as a concession to his age — he would be cooking for many fewer mouths than in a logging camp and living a less regimented life in a beautiful place. He had his own quarters — a walled — off room with a window in a far corner of the kitchen, a privilege of rank. He never had — or at any rate never manifested — any doubts at all about his own importance. Of all the CIP employees and executives I met that summer, he was the only one who lorded it over his subordinates. I was not directly in the line of fire; Maurice was.

On that first afternoon at Lac de La Grosse Ile, after putting my duffle bag in the bunkroom I would share with the guides and Maurice, I walked out to look around.

The camp stood on a knoll, in a natural clearing of eight or ten acres at the end of a long, southward facing cove. Looking down the cove I could see the main body of the lake, which was several miles long and perhaps half a mile wide. All of the buildings were genuine log cabins: peeled and weather-darkened spruce logs carefully notched and fitted. The smaller ones, where the sports stayed, were 25 or 30 feet long, low at the eaves, and relatively wide. Bunks were tucked back under the sloping roof, a snug and pleasant arrangement. In the middle each cabin had a table and chairs, on the rear wall there was a sink and a shelf for dishes, pots, pans, and so forth. It was a short walk to the outhouses. I believe there were four of these cabins. They were in a neat row, well back from the lake. Inside, they had no ceiling, which gave them an airy, open feeling. They were floored and roofed with softwood planking. They had four small windows, two on either side of the front door, and two opposite them, at the back of the cabin. A small woodstove sat toward the back of each camp, with a woodbox beside it. A fifth cabin of the same proportions but without the built-in bunks, had a long table and served as the sports' dining hall.

The other buildings were larger and farther back from the water. There was an icehouse and an equipment shed, which contained the camp's generator, its water pump, and any number of hand tools — shovels, axes, scythes, brush hooks; tools for carpentry; screwdrivers, wrenches, pliers, calipers, gauges, etc. for maintaining and repairing gasoline engines. You could tell it was a well-used place. There was a heavy plank running along one side, where the outboard motors were hung at the end of the season, and quite a collection of steel traps of various sizes on the wall behind it.

A portable sawmill was set up on a back corner of the knoll, with a fair-sized sawdust heap beside it. It could be towed by the camp pickup, and I assume probably spent its winters under cover at a nearby logging camp. There was the kitchen, conveniently close to the sports' dining hall. The bunkhouse where the guides, Maurice, and I stayed and the mess hall where we ate were attached to the kitchen.

Immediately around the cabins and the cookhouse the vegetation had been scythed into a rough, shaggy sort of lawn. The remainder of the clearing was knee deep in bracken ferns, with blueberry bushes scattered among them. There was a line of doorless, south-facing woodsheds along the back edge of the clearing, and well-worn paths between them, the kitchen, and the sports' cabins. Most of the waterfront was a coarse sand and pebble beach that extended well beyond the clearing. Three streams came down to it. They were small and obviously seasonal, ankle-deep and very cold, as I ascertained by accidentally stepping into one, almost invisible down in the bracken.

At supper in the mess hall that night I found that the guides spoke a sort of French — something like a patois. We were able to communicate to the extent of asking, in my bad French or theirs, the man beside or across from us to pass the salt. The guides were neither friendly or unfriendly. I would leave the camp two weeks later knowing almost nothing about them beyond their names. Even among themselves, they had an impassive taciturnity and remoteness. I thought of the nursery rhyme about the wise old owl that sat in the oak: the more he heard, the less he spoke, the less he spoke, the more he heard. The guides all seemed a good deal like that wise old bird. I could not detect any difference in their behavior toward Maurice, the cook, the sports with whom they went out fishing each day, and upon whom they depended for tips, or even toward Emile, who was their boss and was also a man thoroughly at home in their world.

Toward the end of the meal, Maurice came out of the kitchen for a quick bite before going over to serve the sports in their dining hall. Insofar as life in the Deep North went, he was my mentor for the next two weeks. On my first day there, I learned he was from La Tuque and that he was not named for the river. He was Maurice *fils*; Maurice *pere* worked in the paper mill. Neither of them liked it when some wiseacre addressed them as *St. Maurice*. It disrespected them and also the saint and martyr for whom Maurice *pere* had been named. The whole family were serious church-goers. Maurice's elder brother had finished his first year in the seminary at Laval, and two of his uncles had taken Holy Orders and were down in the States. He and his three younger sisters were the only children still at home. He missed them, especially his youngest sister, who wrote him every week to tell him all the news.

Maurice always spoke English to me — so much for improving my French. He said he wanted the practice. Speaking it well would give him a leg up, help him get a better job. He would never be smart enough to learn Latin and follow his brother into the Church, and besides, although he had much admiration for that life, it was not for him. He liked it out here in the bush. But his boss, Gil, the cook, was a hard man to work for, always finding fault, making him do things over. The food here was different from what it was in the logging camps. A lot of it was flown up from Montreal — fresh fruit for pies, fresh vegetables, lamb chops, sometimes even live lobsters, although only the sports got to eat them. He'd never even seen a lobster anywhere else, let alone tasted one. At that point in my life, neither had I.

Between meals, while Gil crapped out on his cot or in his big chair beside the stove, Maurice was free to knock around outside. He liked to be busy. Emile, he said, could do anything — fly a plane or tune and service its engine; build a log cabin that was as neat and comfortable as any house in town, live off the land, speak three languages — French, Cree, and English. And he was a nice guy — took an interest in Maurice, asked him about his family and his plans. Emile would put in a word for him when the cook retired. Maurice was sure of it.

The sports never arrived by the road from La Tuque. Most of them flew in aboard a de Havilland Beaver from Three Rivers, Quebec City, or Montreal, usually arriving early in the afternoon. Their arrivals and departures were the great events of the week. Maurice and I first made sure their camps were swept out and their woodboxes filled. Then we went down to the floating dock, to steady the plane when it pulled in and hold it while the sports stepped out. Most carried their own luggage up to the camps. Maurice and I carried the fresh food. Some of it went directly to the kitchen, but most to the icehouse.

I had never seen an unrefrigerated icehouse before. This one was double-walled, and half buried, with a bulkhead entrance, like a cellar. The walls, about a foot apart, were made of notched logs, with sawdust packed between them. Blocks of ice, cut from the lake in the winter, were kept in a big icebox, and the whole structure was full of snow, shoveled in through a trapdoor in the roof. In June, that snow was still granular. One of our jobs was to clean whatever trout got brought in from fishing, open the icehouse trapdoor, and lay them on top of the snow, like fish on the shaved ice of a fancy seafood store. Before the sports flew home, we'd wrap their fish in brown paper, tape and label it and put it in an ice chest in the Beaver's luggage compartment.

Maurice was thin-faced, tall, skinny, redheaded, and freckled, with large gray-green eyes. He was voluble and utterly unguarded. He used a short, sharp exhalation of breath, something like a rushed whistle, as a sort of exclamation point, as in *"Phew!* Windy today!"* or "Gil —*phew!*— what a shit!" He threw himself into whatever he was doing. Any employer except Gil would be happy to have him and afraid of losing him. He was smitten by the float planes. This would be his third summer in camp, and by now he knew most of the pilots. They teased him and encouraged his fantasies of one day becoming a pilot himself.

The de Havilland Beaver was Maurice's favorite. It was indeed a handsome item: blunt-nosed, sturdy, powerful — 450 horsepower — and capacious. It was built for STOL — short takeoff and landing — and carrying big loads. It could accommodate up to six passengers plus a thousand pounds or so of cargo. In winter, skis replaced the pontoons, and the Beavers kept on truckin' — taking foresters, guides, hunters, trappers, and cross-country skiers wherever they wanted to go. They were icons of the Deep North, replacing the dog team and the canoe in their indispensability, and were eventually featured on a Canadian postage stamp and on the reverse side of a special issue Canadian quarter.

The Beavers normally brought up a 55-gallon drum full of gasoline in the cargo bay, which was to the rear of the passenger compartment. The bay had doors on both sides, so that it could be unloaded on the lee side of the dock whichever way the wind was blowing. The pilot and co-pilot would hop out, moor the plane fore and aft, and snug it in tight against the dock. Then they and a bystander — always Maurice if he were there; it not, me or one of the sports who'd come on the plane — would help them wrestle the drum out of the hold and onto a heavy-duty hand truck. Then it was no problem to roll the truck down the dock and up a ramp to a higher dock, this one set on pilings at the edge of the shore. There was a row of drums on it— fuel for float planes, the camp's big, ¾-ton pick-up, the 15-horse outboards that were used to take sports to distant parts of the lake, and for all the camp's other machinery, including the portable sawmill and a big generator. And for our float plane, a Cessna Skyhawk, moored at the dock. It was used to carry a sport or two, a guide, and a canoe to one of the ponds or lakes nearby. And it was there in case of emergencies, when somebody might need to get to a hospital in a hurry, or when a sport had to leave early because some important business or personal matter had come up back in civilization.

Before the Beaver left to return to civilization, we would load any empty 55-gallon drums into the cargo bay. Often by that time of day, heavy swells and whitecaps would be rolling into our cove. I never saw the pilots show any hesitation or concern. Once any departing sports and their luggage were aboard, they taxied out, pointed the nose into the wind and opened the throttle. The mighty engine roared, the plane threw up heavy spray as it pounded across the waves and in no time it was aloft, hardly making forward progress against the wind but gaining altitude, clearing the tree line and the low ridges, then heeling over and heading for home — Three Rivers, Montreal, or Quebec — another day's work done.

When only one or two sports came up, they usually arrived in Cessnas like the one we had. The Cessnas were sleeker in their lines and had fancy paint jobs — more like sports cars than pickup trucks. The Beaver was the emblematic plane of the north, and the pride of Canadian aeronautical engineering, but the Cessnas were the taxicabs. Anywhere up there, if you heard a plane overhead and looked up, nine times out of ten you'd see a Cessna.

Emile Richard, the boss, had his own cabin, which doubled as the camp office. It was the first building Andrew and I had passed as we drove into camp and was somewhat taller than the sports' cabins. His sleeping quarters were upstairs, in a loft. Downstairs, he had his own kitchen and sink, a small table, and a filing cabinet. I have the impression that he lived there year-round, partly to keep an eye on things, but also because the bush was his natural habitat.

Emile wasn't in the least bossy. He was soft-spoken, omnicompetent, unhurried, and perhaps in his mid-fifties. He knew most of the sports from previous visits. In a corporate world defined by hierarchies of wealth, power, educational status, professional accomplishment, and so forth, they far outranked him. He ran a small sporting camp. Within the CIP hierarchy, that ranked him well above being a woodcutter, a camp cook, timber cruiser, or heavy machinery operator, but he was still more or less analogous to a non-commissioned officer, as far below the head honchos back at the home office — CEOs, CFOs, vice presidents in charge of public relations, corporate recruitment, etc. — as a master sergeant is below a brigadier, major, or lieutenant general. But the CIP executives at Grosse Ile did not behave themselves like big shots on vacation, among people being paid to cater to them, amuse them, feed them, and clean up after them. They acted instead as though they were the personal guests of Emile Richard. I thought that was admirable. I do not know whether it says more about the corporate culture of CIP, the civilization of Canada, or Emile's quiet, innate authority.

It now occurs to me that Emile Richard was the spiritual and very possibly the literal descendant of the *coureurs du bois* of Quebec, who from the 17th century onward had defied French efforts to limit the lucrative fur trade to officially authorized agents on the one hand, and indigenous people on the other. The *coureurs du bois* had taken to the woods, away from all the high-feudal folderol of New France, to trap and trade for themselves among the natives, and in many cases to marry into the tribes and raise their children in the native manner. Emile spoke French and English with equal ease, but he spoke them softly, in a cadence that did not seem typical of either. He was never hurried, and even when doing fussy jobs — taking apart the carburetor of one of the outboards or painting the trim on a cabin — he seemed off-hand, like a man whose thoughts were elsewhere.

As Andrew Stevens had predicted, he found a lot for me to do. I was not handy with scythes but had had plenty of practice with a brush hooks and a sling blades. There was always firewood to be bucked up and split; there were paths — one went back to the garbage heap; another, much longer, went to a smaller pond where a couple of canoes were stashed, a good place for sports to fish on windy days, and I was given clippers and a bucksaw and set to cutting back the spruce limbs to widen the path. It was buggy work, but it offered shelter from the ferocious brilliance and glare of being out in the open and down by the water. A few times, I drove the truck down to the main road to meet the bush bus and pick up things Gil had ordered for the kitchen — usually staples like flour, butter, eggs, bacon, beans, onions, and potatoes.

When you are in a new place and busy, the passage of time very quickly disconnects from the calendar. Nothing at Lac de La Grosse Ile distinguished Mondays from Tuesdays, or weekends from the week. I am sure it was different for Emile, who had to keep track of which sports were arriving when, and what necessities were running low. Because I was outside all day, and always occupied, there was no need for me to pull my watch out of my pocket. Gil would strike the iron triangle announcing that breakfast, dinner, or supper was being served, and then I would stop what I was doing and go in. I would not notice that I had been hungry until I began to eat.

One day stood out from the rest. If I had not found the cache of letters I wrote home, I would tell you it came after I'd been at Lac de La Grosse Ile for at least a week. But in fact, it happened on my fourth night there. Started the evening before that, actually.

Most of the sports who came up in June, strictly for the fishing, preferred to fish with cut bait out in the lake. They'd put a piece of sucker on a hook attached to a heavy single-bladed spinner, lower it to the bottom, and jig it up and down. Normally, they fished from an anchored outboard skiff, so they could move quickly from one spot to another. The guides knew where the deep holes and productive ledges were. The sports in June were looking for big fish, perhaps trophies. One or two of those hung on the walls of their dining hall — brook trout that weighed five or six pounds. The best ones caught while I was there were a pair brought in on my last evening in camp. Nobody bothered to weigh them. They were probably three pounds apiece, more or less — respectable but not remarkable.

Back when Emile and a crew were building the camp, a decade or so earlier, they had taken a late summer afternoon off from hammering and sawing, and Emile had used dynamite to blast a big hole in one of the streams that ran out of the woods through the bracken to the beach. The hole was only a short way back from the beach itself. To concentrate the water that flowed over the lip of the pond and across the beach, they built a spillway, defined by levees of rock and sand. Each winter, ice and high water destroyed the levee and filled the pond with sand, but when the water receded it was a simple matter to dig the hole out again and rebuild the levee. Now, with the water in the lake having receded farther, we went out after supper and extended the levee ten or fifteen feet into knee-deep water. The larger rocks we prized up still had frost clinging to their undersides. It was a still, overcast evening. Maurice said that was good — suckers were skittish about coming up into skinny water on bright, moonlit nights. The water was bitterly cold; my hands and feet were numb.

We were through by about ten o'clock, with the long summer twilight still illuminating the water and the sand. It made the lights of the camp softer than they would appear a half hour later, when something like final darkness closed down.

Next morning, Maurice, Emile, and two of the guides, Alexi and Peter, and I went back to the beach at the first lifting of darkness, about 3:30. Emile went up to the pond, moving quietly. The rest of us took the seine out into the lake and stood a little way back from the lower end of the levee, keeping still and quiet. There were still suckers entering the spillway, swimming on their sides until they reached the lip of the pond, floundered over it, and disappeared.

Emile raised his hand, and we spread the seine across the lower end of the levee. Then he started thrashing the surface of the pond with a stick. The fish rushed back down toward the lake, and in a matter of seconds the seine was bulging with them. It was all we could do to drag it up to the beach. The suckers heaved and flopped, coating themselves with sand. We folded the seine over them and walked up to the mess hall. Gil had had to get up early but he was almost cheerful as he served us the usual breakfast — fresh baked bread, scrambled eggs, good thick-sliced bacon, hash-browned potatoes. Nobody talked much — we needed to get back to the fish — but everybody was happy.

We took two scalers and two thin-bladed kitchen knives, honed very sharp, from Gil's kitchen. A couple of ravens were standing on the seine, stabbing their beaks through the mesh and trying to worry out gobbets of fish flesh. Several others stood around on the beach. Alexi and Peter brought down a table— planks nailed together—that sat on a pair of sawhorses, and we got to work, two scaling and two filleting. We weren't fussy about the filleting, leaving a good deal of meat on the skeleton. Then we cut the fillets into bait-sized chunks, put them in a cloth bag, and put it in the icehouse. We had enough bait to last at least a month, by which time the sucker run would be over. The guides would stop by the icehouse each morning, taking only enough bait for that day's fishing, and throwing the unused portion of it overboard at the end of the day.

When we were finished, Maurice and I carried the tabletop with the fish heads, guts, and skeletons on it to the garbage pile. It was abuzz with blue-bottle flies, and a few ravens were pecking around. We dumped the whole mess onto the pile. Before we left, Alexi came up from the camp carrying a bear trap. He didn't put the trap directly onto the heap — for one thing, a raven would probably trip it; for another, if you did get a bear, it would be a filthy, malodorous mess by the time you got it out of the trap. Instead, Alexi took the trap down a path that was obviously used regularly by bears—their dung and tracks were all along it. He set it between two big logs that lay across the path and cocked it. Contrary to everything I'd read about trappers and trapping, he made no effort to conceal his scent. The animals that came here were used to the smell — the stink of humanity was just a part of the olfactory background. He sprinkled leaves and twigs over the trap, shackled it to the base of a small spruce, and we left.

Maurice explained there was a ten-dollar bounty on bears, but only Indians were eligible for it. They had to scalp the bear and present the scalp, with both ears attached, to the proper official. I don't know whether the official had to be a game warden or was merely the director of any of CIP's logging or sporting camps. I'm guessing the latter. Even if they had incinerators, all camps were bound to attract bears, and bears could do a lot of damage—break into storerooms, icehouses, and almost any place else. I have the impression that bounty money was shared equally among the guides at the end of the season. I'm guessing that Emile collected the scalps and dispensed the money.

In the event, later that afternoon, we heard squalling and thrashing in the woods, and there was a bear in the trap. He might have weighed forty pounds. Peter, another of the guides, went back to the bunkhouse and returned with a rifle. The little bear saw us approaching—the squalling had been caused by pain; the noise it made now—louder and more like bawling— was caused by terror.

I'd seen raccoons in traps a time or two at home, and it was a sad sight, the animal plainly terrified, snarling, its back all humped up and its tail fluffed out like a bottle brush. But bears are much more human, and not simply because they stand on their hind legs. Even compared to dogs, their emotions and re- actions seem closer to ours. Peter levelled the gun, sighted care- fully, and shot. The animal died all at once, in a heap. Peter took it out of the trap, and I went over to look at it. It was scruffy and scrawny—no trace remaining of the plump cuteness of a cub. Peter roped its forepaws together and dragged it back to camp. He would need to scalp it. I didn't learn what happened to the carcass of that bear or the one that blundered into the same trap a few days later. The two of them looked like identical twins— both males, both about the size of a gawky five-year old boy with unusually thick and muscular arms and legs. Possibly Emile stowed them in the icehouse and kept them until he could turn them over to the Canadian Wildlife Service, for whatever studies they wanted to conduct.

This teeming, concentrated fecundity of the Deep North at the end of winter was not anything my reading had prepared me for. It was an atmosphere you inhaled and incorporated. Despite three big meals a day, I was always hungry when the next one was put before me; and even with the short nights, I never felt drowsy. There were fish, insects, the blundering and hapless adolescent bears, and especially there were birds. Some were entirely new to me—loons, spruce grouse, crossbills, ravens, Canada jays, and a northern shrike that perched all day on the electric line that ran from the generator to the camps. Occasionally it fluttered down to the rough lawn and caught a beetle or vole, and once a junco. Even familiar birds like the robins that hung around the camp clearing looked bigger and brighter than the ones in South Carolina. But the biggest difference was in the neotropical migrants—warblers and kinglets that wintered in South Carolina or passed through in the spring and fall. I almost never saw them there, where even the ones that wintered over were silent and reclusive. Up here, in their full breeding colors, busy marking out their territories and mating, they were easy to see, easy to hear. I did not need to go looking for them and I did not need binoculars or a field guide to see and identify them. Which was just as well, because I had not brought either of those things with me. Memory served.

Many years later, the great naturalist E.O. Wilson would coin the term *biophilia* to describe a deep-seated affinity, like the social instinct, that attracts us to all biological life. Because I have wound up living the whole of my adult life in Maine, with its drastic seasons, the rapid lengthening of the days after about the middle of February has become for me as inseparable from the impending onset of creaturely life as music is from a parade. Northern Quebec in early June was my first, and most intense, encounter with that, and it awakened something akin to a migratory instinct in me, a paradoxical kind of northward yearning, to prolong the season of budding and blooming, to stay just ahead of the arrivals of waterfowl, swallows, thrushes, and warblers. South Carolina had a greater fecundity than Maine or Quebec; and Costa Rica and Belize, when I visited them years later, had a variety and ubiquity of trees and critters far exceeding even that of the Carolina lowcountry, but I had no desire at all ever to live in South Carolina again, or to stay for more than a week or two at a time in Central America. With their muted seasonal rhythms, they were like seas that had only negligible tides, or no tides at all.

As for my northward yearnings: after two weeks at the fishing camp, I said goodbye to the guides and Emile. Maurice drove me out to the primary road which ran north from La Tuque and left me there with my duffle bag — he had to get back to the kitchen to begin fixing the midday meal.

The bush bus — an ordinary school bus—picked me up in the early afternoon. On the seat behind the driver there was a big pouch, full of incoming and outgoing mail; farther back were a variety of boxes and cartons. These contained supplies for particular camps along the line: perhaps food, perhaps the variety of items — everything from steel-toed boots to postage stamps and over-the-counter medications — that were sold in the camp commissaries. Mail pick-up and delivery required the driver to turn off the main road and go into each camp, a mile or two into the woods. My memory of that first trip on the bush bus is overlaid by three subsequent ones. In the middle of the summer timber cruisers and compass men got a three-day paid vacation in La Tuque. We stayed at the Windsor Hotel, at no charge, and paid for our own food and drink. Our last trip down was at the end of August. Most, or possibly all, of us were college students, and had to get back for the beginning of the fall semester.

Except for the first trip, I was among friends, and did not pay much attention to the camps or take notice of the *bucherons*. What follows is an imprecise impression, augmented by speculation.

The first thing you saw as you pulled into a CIP logging camp was a three-story barracks, in which the *bucherons* slept and had their meals. There was always a sign in front of it: THIS CAMP HAS WORKED ____ DAYS WITHOUT AN ACCIDENT. Two weeks seemed to be about the average. "Accident" presumably meant an injury serious enough to require the worker to be evacuated to La Tuque. Lesser cuts, bruises, and sprains could be treated with medications and first aid supplies from the commissary and involved no loss of man-hours.

To the extent that "barracks" implies a military context, it is the right word—a CIP logging camp resembled an army base, both in itself and in its being part of an enormous, interconnected operation. The buildings in each camp were more or less the same and were arranged in more or less the same fashion. They were not constructed of logs — they had conventional framing and corrugated metal siding. The administrators of the camp had a separate building, which contained not only the offices but living and sleeping quarters. In addition to the buildings that housed the camp's personnel, there was an array of outbuildings: big sheds, where skidders, front end loaders, bulldozers, graders, back hoes were kept; metal-working and repair shops; a fuel depot and, some distance from it, pumps like ordinary filling station pumps, one for diesel and one for gas. There was obviously a large generator somewhere and a well and a water-pump somewhere else. Electrical, fuel, and power lines were evidently buried, and all of the sheds were enclosed to keep out snow in the winter, and perhaps to keep out bugs and dust in summer. The overall effect was in no way pleasing, but it did indicate the vast scale of CIP's operation, its great financial resources and its efficiency in deploying them.

The purpose of a logging camp was simple—to allow the *bucherons* to live in proximity to the trees they were cutting. Each time I traveled to or from Cooper Lake, I slept one night in the barracks at one camp, and had my supper and my breakfast there, and always had my midday meal — dinner — at another camp. I have no memory at all of how often we pulled into other camps along the way.

Back in the spring, when I was already planning to go north to improve my French, the FLQ — Front de Liberation du Quebec — began making news. There had been the bombing of a military barracks in Montreal. The FLQ was Marxist-Leninist in its ideology, practiced terrorism as a means of propaganda, and aimed for the establishment an independent Quebec, French in language and culture. Its most proximate inspiration was probably Castro's Cuba, but in the United States analogies between it and the Civil Rights movement, just now getting under way, were irresistible. I knew where I stood on that issue and had read enough Marx to be vaguely Marxist/Socialist in my economic views. And I had been struck by the way in which people like Andrew Stevens and Maurice spoke of *bucherons*. It did not have the pseudo-Darwinian, visceral revulsion of racism, but was more akin to the way more or less gentrified and educated southerners (and indeed, Americans in general) spoke of poor rural whites as *rednecks* or, more genteelly but no less patronizingly, as *the salt of the earth*. I'd hoped, through conversation or observation, to get at least some sense of how the *bucherons* felt about the FLQ, about the secessionist movement in Quebec, and about CIP.

But in fact, I learned nothing about them, not even whether they were directly employed by CIP or whether they were crews provided to CIP by subcontractors in La Tuque, Three Rivers, and elsewhere in French Canada. All, so far as I could tell, were exclusively francophone. All seemed very much acculturated to life in the logging camp, which doesn't mean that they liked it, only that they assented to its rules and regulations, the rhythms of the workday and the week, the living quarters they inhabited and the food they ate. The greatest of their deprivations must have been their distance from friends, family, neighbors, gossip, recreation — all the things that are the warp and the woof of life in an ordinary community. Thinking about them now, I believe that each man was a member of a regular crew, that always worked together; that they signed on for a fixed term — so many weeks or months at a stretch; and that wherever they lived when not in the bush, they were connected to each other by family, neighborhood, or long acquaintance. Between their stints in the bush, they probably picked up income doing this or that — plowing snow, splitting wood, perhaps taking some relatively unspecialized job in one of CIP's mills.

In the evenings, at supper, they ate rather more deliberately than they did the following morning, chatted more, and occasionally laughed. Nobody appeared to be in a rush, but, as at all their meals, they ate in a workman-like fashion, not voraciously, like dogs, or mincingly, like cats, but methodically and unhurriedly, like draft animals. They were not at all in the heroic, big-talking tradition of Paul Bunyan, Mike Finn, or the stereotypical frontiersman, nor were they given to macho bawdy, obscenity, or profanity.

They generally conformed to a single body-type: long-waisted and short-legged, like Maine lobstermen, most baseball catchers, and Humphrey Bogart. Sitting at the table, they looked taller than they were. CIP regulations required them to wear canvas pants, with heavy duty nylon thigh pads sewn into them, canvas work shirts, leather work gloves, steel-toed boots, and, of course, hard hats. The hard hats had steel mesh screens to protect their eyes against sawdust. This amounted to a uniform, but given the nature of their work, the shirts and pants were ragged and patched, gummy with pitch from the trees and stained by grease. They were as neat in their habits as it was possible to be, but pitch doesn't scrub off easily. Their hands were almost black with it.

As for their work: I never actually saw a cutting operation. They left after breakfast in a large van, carrying their saws with them. Unless the crew was cutting quite close to the camp, a dinner was provided for them. I doubt it could have been nearly as good as the midday meals that were served in the mess hall, but from my subsequent experience, I'm certain that the food would have been copious and nourishing and would have included bread baked that morning. CIP wanted its workers to be well-fed and well-housed; and insofar as possible, it sought to make their inherently dangerous work less dangerous. But of course, it also wanted them to be as productive as possible. My guess is that their paychecks reflected not only how many hours they had worked, but how many cords of pulpwood they had felled, bucked up, and stacked. To the extent that this rewarded speed, it increased fatigue and the likelihood of accident.

At that point in my life, I'd never owned or operated a chainsaw, and knew absolutely nothing about them. I assume, but do not know, that CIP purchased its saws in bulk; that it chose the most reliable models of the best brands, got them at a big discount, and had factory-trained repairmen to overhaul them. It is quite likely that Canada already had something akin to the Logger Certification Program that Maine instituted thirty years later, emphasizing both worker safety and sound forestry practices. But the finest chainsaw on the market in 1963 would have been significantly heavier and much more dangerous than even a bargain-basement model bought from a big box store in an outlet mall today. In 1963, chain saws did not have chain brakes or vibration-reducing systems. Kickback, which the chain brake was designed to prevent, would certainly have been the commonest source of serious accidents in the camps, and would have inflicted ugly cuts in upper arms, shoulders, or face. The undampered vibration of the saw would greatly increase fatigue to the hands and wrist, making the saw that much more danger-ous, and it could over time cause permanent damage to the joints, tendons, and nerves.

Whatever their terms of employment and backgrounds were, I felt sure that they would regard me as an Anglo Yank who had benefitted from insider connections to land a job with CIP, thereby taking it away from a Canadian, and who now got to eat the wonderful, sustaining food at their table, to sleep in their comfortable, tidy barracks at night, and to spend a summer in the remoter depths of the Deep North as a paid tourist.

The overhead lights in the dormitory turned off at some point in the evening. It hardly mattered. After supper, some of the men showered, some did not. Then they got into their bunks, and within minutes were snoring, although it was still light outside. I must have fallen asleep pretty quickly myself. They had had another in a long series of exhausting days. I had not, but it didn't seem to matter. I do not remember any sort of breakfast bell the next morning, only sitting at the long table again. Eating was a serious business. One spoke to one's neighbor only to ask him to pass the salt or coffee. My French was sufficient for that, and in all likelihood their English would have been. But in terms of etiquette, to talk further would have been like striking up a conversation with a stranger who happened to be seated next to you in church.

COOPER LAKE: *PLOT, CLUSTER, AND FLY*

That much, then, by way of the socioeconomic and political context of my summer. It came briefly into focus in the logging camps, but as soon as I reached Cooper Lake, it evaporated. What followed did nothing for my French but was the finest kind of educational experience, not merely informative but formative.

The camp at Cooper Lake, which served as my base of operations for the next two months, is much less distinct in my memory than the fishing camp. My recollection is of a large, open, grassy hillside. The cruisers and compass men were housed in something like a college dormitory — two to a room, bathrooms with shower stalls down the hall, and a dining area downstairs. There were a couple dozen of us in all. The majority spoke French, and most, if not all, of them were enrolled in undergraduate forestry programs. CIP offered summer internships for students in those programs. The first year, they would work as compass men, the second as cruisers. Their courses would have given them the skills they needed for the work.

Life at Cooper Lake was not controlled by the clock or the calendar. Everything depended on the weather, and, weather permitting, we spent very little time in our quarters there, or at the lake at all. As far as I know, the place had only a single purpose, which was to oversee and tabulate the results of CPI's forestry monitoring program. Their lease required it. As we understood it, someone back in Montreal, or perhaps in Ottawa, had more or less thrown darts at a very large map of CPI's leasehold. A cruiser and compass man would go to each spot thus selected, paddling to a point on the shoreline designated on an ariel photograph, and from there following a prescribed compass course a certain distance, measured in chains, and mark off a circular *plot*.

Each plot was one chain — 66 feet — in radius. As a compass man, I had a pint-sized, manually operated paint gun in my backpack, a cloth tape measure in my pocket, and a surveyor's chain; I would attach my end to my belt, while the cruiser held its opposite end. I would paint a number 1 on the closest tree to where I stood, measure its diameter breast high, and call that out. Tom, my cruiser, would record it in his tally book. Then he would release his end of the chain, and I would attach it to tree #1 and begin making my way clockwise around the plot, numbering each tree, measuring it, and calling that information out to Tom. When every tree was numbered, measured, and tallied, Tom, using a Biltmore stick — something like an ordinary yardstick but a bit longer and a bit more substantial — would measure the height of every fourth tree. His last job was to use a corer to ascertain the age of tree #1, the one standing at the center of the circle. He did not attempt to count the growth rings, but carefully put the core sample into a plastic tube like an ordinary drinking straw, clipped it shut, labelled it and put it in a special pouch. Back in Montreal, the growth rings would be counted and analyzed under a microscope. This would not only reveal the age of the tree but also its rate of growth from year to year.

When finished with that plot, we followed a predetermined compass bearing for ten chains — a quarter of a mile — to the next one, and repeated the whole drill, numbering, measuring, and recording. Then we continued on that same compass bearing another quarter mile, to a third plot. A group of three plots like this was called a *cluster*. And a cluster was our day's work. At the third plot, I could reel in the chain, and we could follow a fixed compass bearing back to the lake. If we'd done everything right, we'd come out exactly where we'd left the canoe, paddle back to camp, and have the rest of the day to ourselves.

Ten years later, another cruiser and compass man would revisit each plot in each cluster, and repeat all the measurements we had made, tree by tree. They could ascertain the growth rate of each tree over the past decade, make notes about any signs of serious disturbance, by fire, disease, heavy wind, etc. It was nice to think that the tiny marks we had left in the middle of all this wilderness would be relocated, and the individual trees would again be found. Because otherwise, there was almost no sign of human presence in those thousands and thousands of square miles.

Each expedition out from Cooper Lake was called a *fly*. Tom was from Toronto but majoring in forestry at the University of New Brunswick. The pilot who normally flew us out to our camp site was Claude. He was French Canadian and very cool — wrap-around sunglasses, brown hair slicked back and carefully combed, and fond of brightly printed shirts, peg-legged trousers, and white, canvas-soled deck shoes. His English was good. Tom and I sat on the back seats; a 17' or 18' Chestnut wood-canvas canoe was lashed between the pontoons, and behind us, our camping gear and food were packed into a luggage compartment, which was about the size of the trunk of an ordinary mid-sized sedan. I have absolutely no memory of packing the gear and the food. It was always done for us, by somebody who had a checklist, and knew precisely where and how each item on it should be stowed. We never unpacked at our campsite to find that something necessary had been left back at Cooper Lake.

I know nothing about aerial navigation. I assume that the Cessna's instrument panel allowed Claude to set a compass course and follow it to the lake that had been selected as our camping site — that is, the lake within convenient distance, by canoe and on foot, of the maximum number of clusters. Wherever possible, the designated spot would have a beach, so that the Cessna could glide gently up to it and allow us to offload our gear without scrambling up a rocky foreshore. And wherever possible, there would be a relatively treeless area for pitching the tent.

The instrument panel would have also let Claude know his ground speed and elevation. And he had beside him on the seat a looseleaf binder with aerial photographs of the landscape we would fly over on our way to our landing site. Lakes, rivers, and ponds showed clearly; he could glance down and see exactly where he was and, by looking at the surface of the lakes, see what the wind was doing. His general lounge-lizard affect was misleading — he was all business in the air, and especially when we reached our destination and prepared to land. He would circle the lake very carefully. He had no information whatsoever about what it was like below the surface. If it was windy, there was no chance of seeing a rock or a waterlogged tree trunk just below the surface. Dead calm conditions were better, in terms of visibility, but they were also rare. Once on the water, the pilot had no forward visibility until the plane settled and the nose came down. Then he could taxi at an idle toward the shore. Crosswinds could make that difficult. We never once hit anything when we touched down or failed to get the plane to as good a location for offloading as the site allowed, but we did have moments of incipient airsickness as Claude, with the plane banked sharply to the left, to allow him to study the lake, circled, circled, circled, and circled, choosing his spot.

With only one or two exceptions, Tom and I were paired with Bob and Philip. They too were in the undergraduate Forestry program at UNB. Bob, like Tom, had completed his second year, and was a cruiser; Philip, like me, was a compass man, but a compass man whose course work had prepared him specifically for participating in CPI's monitoring program. Claude would fly one pair of us out, then the other. The flight that went out first always had the tent and bedding in it, and enough canned food to last a couple of days — if the weather took a sudden turn for the worse, Claude might not be able to come back for a day or two. As it turned out, that never happened, but it was typical of how carefully things were thought out.

Our tent and bedding typified something else, and I am not sure what it was. The tent was a wall tent, very roomy — perhaps ten feet long and eight wide. To erect it we first staked out the 8x10 footprint of the tent, using a tape measure and making it as true a rectangle as we could. Then we cut down seven conifers of six to eight inches in diameter, sawed them into 12-foot lengths, trimmed off the branches, and made them into a frame from which to suspend the tent. We first lashed two logs together, roughly two feet from their ends, making a lopsided X, then we did the same with another pair of logs. We placed their butt ends at the corners of the footprint and staked them into place. Then we raised them, using an improvised plumbline to make them as vertical as possible, and temporary guy lines to keep them erect. After that, we laid the ridgepole between them, lashed it down, and then two side poles, about waist high. When those were tightly lashed, our frame was reasonably rigid. The tent hung inside it. A fly ran over the ridgepole and the two side poles and was pegged tight to the ground. The fly was water-proofed; the tent itself was not. There was space for air to circulate between the fly and the tent, which cooled things on hot days and kept things perfectly dry on rainy ones.

It was a lot of work. When done, the tent was about as comfortable as a tent could be — plenty big enough to move around in, between six and seven feet high beneath the ridgepole. But the tent would have made more sense if we had been planning to stay in one place for several weeks, or even the whole summer. It was true that stays could be prolonged by bad weather: we could not do the job if there was a steady rain. Even so, we never stayed in one place more than a week.

Our mattresses were made of dense, inch-thick felt, six feet long by two feet wide. I had never seen or heard of camping mattresses like that. They were heavy even when perfectly dry; they could not be folded, only rolled into a clumsy cylinder; and, while comfortable enough, had no obvious superiority to foam rubber, which was ten times lighter, could be rolled into a much more compact cylinder, and would have been less expensive. The felt seemed like a nineteenth-century technology, one that ought to have gone the way of the grandfather clock and the chamber pot.

Our cooking was done on a collapsible, short-legged box stove. The cooking surface was about 2' x 1', the stove pipe was 4' long, 6" in diameter, with a spark arrestor at the top. Prior to setting it up, we were required to dig out, as best we could, a rectangular hole, removing all vegetation in the process, and then fill it with small stones, to create a kind of hearth. CIP very properly insisted on the utmost care in handling anything that involved open flame. We were absolutely forbidden to have campfires, even on wide, sandy beaches well away from the woods. We were permitted to smoke only hand-rolled cigarettes, and to smoke them only when sitting or standing, never when moving. All matches had to be pinched out and broken in half before being discarded. At the cookstove, we were always to have a two-gallon pot of water close at hand as a fire extinguisher.

Nick Adams, after a hot walk in to the Big Two-Hearted River, pitches his tent, which smells pleasantly of canvas, and places his gear inside. He notices that "Already there was something mysterious and homelike" about it. Before going out to cook his supper, he savors a sensation which I think any camper will recognize: "He was in his home where he had made it." If you are beside some large, nameless lake in northern Quebec, where you've erected your big tent frame, hung and pegged down your tent, built your outdoor kitchen, with improvised log stools or benches so that you can sit with your plate in your lap, eat, and talk; and have done that for a week, in the process wearing several trails — one down to the rock at the edge of the lake where you scoop up water for cooking and washing; another to where the canoes lie overturned and tied down, waiting for you to come down to them like a commuter to his car right after breakfast the next morning; a third, back into the woods to a conveniently located log — ideally, a smooth-barked birch — that serves as your *plein air* privy: after a week of that, you unconsciously begin to feel like a naturalized citizen, not just a stranger passing through. Of course, when the time came for us to leave, we could look forward to mail, showers, a proper bed, people to talk to and horse around with, wonderful, substantial northwoods food, and so forth. It was like leaving home at the end of the summer and returning to college.

To me the saddest part of leaving was pulling down our log tent frame. We did it out of thrift — the lashing rope would be needed on our next fly. But if we had left it standing, the stark silhouette of the bare frame would have served for at least a few years as an indication of human presence in a world that had very, very few of them. In all of our canoeing and walking that summer, we saw exactly one habitation: a low, rough log cabin, the logs chinked with moss and the roof of riven spruce shakes overlaid by it. Bob said it was a trapper's cabin for sure. There was a lean-to against one side, with a fair amount of firewood piled against it. And there was a small grove of spruce trees around the cabin that had been girdled, probably last summer, and were now dead on their feet. Bob explained to me that this was in effect a standing woodpile, so the trapper would not have to dig down through the snow to get at his wood. And how deep would the snow cover be? Oh, six feet, give or take.

I believe all CIP's camps north of La Tuque had radio communication with each other and back to La Tuque. But on our flies, we had to rely on very simple signals that would be visible from the air. One band of white cloth stretched across the tent fly meant *All's Well*. Two meant *Work's Done — Pick Us Up*. Three meant *Land at Once: Emergency*. Claude or another pilot from Cooper Lake flew over every tent site on every day when flying was possible. Thinking about it now, this probably indicated that cruisers and compass men from Cooper Lake all worked within a particular quadrant at the same time, perhaps within a few dozen miles of each other. A pilot could complete a fly-over of all the tents within an hour or less, often while on his way to picking up one crew or landing another.

I do not know how far our various camping places were from Cooper Lake. The planes had a cruising speed of about 100 mph. In my recollection, our flights seldom if ever exceeded an hour, but my recollection here may be off. Flying itself was so interesting that I wasn't often conscious of the passage of time. Generally, we flew low enough that, by August, if a moose was standing in a pond, we could tell whether it was a bull, cow or yearling. When we had to climb to cross over high ridges, we got a wider view. From an elevation of perhaps half a mile we could often see CIP clearcuts. We had been told that it would take so long for CIP systematically to clearcut the whole of its lease in Quebec, from south to north and from Ontario to the Maritime Provinces, that the first clearcuts would have reached maturity by the time the last ones were made, and they could simply start all over again, like a man mowing an enormous lawn. I knew enough to know that this kind of argument had been made about the forests of our own North Woods and Wild West and that it was wrong. But from a plane half a mile up, the clearcuts looked insignificant, like so many postage stamps widely scattered over a gymnasium floor.

For all the pleasure and interest of our flights to and from our camp sites, and then in the routines of camp life, those things were peripheral to our daily trips, first by canoe and then on foot, to the sites where we gathered the data that was the point of the whole endeavor. This might involve a long paddle and a short walk, a short paddle and a long walk, or any combination of the two. The canoeing part was generally quicker.

It seemed to be traditional that the cruiser was the stern paddler and the compass man the bow paddler. So, I paddled bow. That allowed me more opportunity to enjoy the scenery and look for wildlife, and also on windy days or small rivers to appreciate how much more maneuverable a canoe was than the small, locally made, wooden johnboats I was accustomed to. The bow paddler could pull the boat sideways, to keep it facing into the wind or to dodge a rock. And a canoe with a pair of more or less competent paddlers in it could handle impressively rough water. Thus, our workdays began and ended with what seemed much more like recreation than like work.

Now that I have better than half a century of canoeing in northern Maine under my belt, what most strikes me about our paddling that summer is how rarely we saw mammals. Only once, on a small, sluggish stream, did we see a moose — a fine, mature cow. It was in August, we rounded a sharp turn, and there she was, belly deep in the water, with her head submerged. We stopped paddling and sat still. She lifted her head, bringing up a skein of dripping water weed. It took her a moment to notice us, but when she did, she snorted and surged out of the stream and into the alders along the bank like a racehorse out of the gate. One moose. Just one for a whole summer in what appeared to be ideal moose habitat. And we never saw a single beaver and only a couple of their lodges. I did not experience this as anything unusual, and nobody commented on it. But it makes me reflect on the possibility that since northern Quebec had a healthy population of indigenous hunter-gatherers; critters — or at least mammals — had every reason to be skittish of the sight or scent of bipeds, afoot or afloat.

Following a predetermined compass course through wooded country is always more laborious than making your way to a predetermined point, but with the freedom to dodge around obstacles and take advantage of the contours of the land. Because I'd worked as a compass man in South Carolina, I knew that. In South Carolina there were thicker thickets and denser woods to contend with; a compass man carried a machete and often needed it. On the other hand, in South Carolina differences in elevation were negligible; in Quebec, they were not.

We basically traversed only two types of woodland: predominantly aspen-birch and predominantly spruce-fir. The latter was far more widespread and might be anywhere. The hardwoods favored slopes, and particularly slopes adjacent to open water. From the canoe, they looked park-like — you could imagine riding a horse through them. Beneath them the ground was typically covered with ferns or bracken. It was very pretty. But it meant you could not see where you were placing your feet. There were a lot of rocks and boulders obstructing your path; a lot of places to bang your shin or twist your ankle. I had to follow an exact compass line. Tom, coming up behind, did not. He could simply drop his end of the chain and follow the path of least resistance, as I reeled in the chain.

Spruce woods have a much denser canopy than birch-aspen woods. The shade beneath them is almost impermeable, and perhaps for that reason sphagnum moss, about shin deep, carpets the ground under them. Beneath your feet, it is spongy, wet, and cool. You'll go over your boots pretty regularly. In your pocket, you carry a collapsible tin cup. On hot days (and midsummer can swelter up there, sweating every drop out of you) you take it out, force it down a few inches into the moss, let the water seep into it. It is cold enough to make your teeth ache. It has a mossy bouquet. Resist the temptation to gulp — you'll give yourself a cramp. Sniff, sip, swirl it around in your mouth, then let it slide down your throat. Take off your hardhat; pour a cupful over your head. Then another, down the back of your neck. Shiver.

I was surprised by how infrequently I had to scramble over a fallen tree or big branches that had been broken off by wind or the weight of snow. Of course, the roots of these trees would be densely intertwined, which would help hold them up, and the same was true of their crowns. All of the woodland was largely free of undergrowth. That, like the absence of fallen trees, enhanced its parklike qualities. You could normally see a long way ahead through the dappled shade. The effect did not at all evoke the sublimity and vistas of the great tradition of American wilderness painting; it called for something intimate, intricate, and enclosed, a chiaroscuro effect: Courbet, the Barbizon School. Blah, blah. It is hard to convey the pleasure of knowing that you were in an utterly wild place that yet had the feeling of the most civilized of all spaces, an exceptionally fine urban or manorial park, like the ones Olmsted designed.

Because we had the aerial photographs, we always had some idea of the kind of terrain we were going to encounter on the way to any particular plot. Muskegs, for example, were obvious, and some of them were big. Once Tom and I dutifully slogged several hundred yards out into one to measure our first plot, then half a mile more along the predetermined compass line to do the other two. At least one of the plots was entirely treeless — not even so much as an alder. The other two had a few spindly black spruce and a larch or two. That was it. We were often knee deep in muck. But it had been impressed upon us that the logic of a random sampling allowed for no cutting of corners. From the knees down, our pants looked, and to some extent smelled, like we'd waded through a septic tank. On the other hand, our day's work was done; it was not yet midmorning, and soon we'd be back in camp, where we could wade out, scour our trousers with sand, and let them dry in the heat of the sun on a rock. After a few hours they were as dry and warm as though they'd been freshly ironed.

A few of our other plots turned out to be located on top of stony cliffs. All our measurements were based on aerial photographs, which show only horizontal distance. Neither Tom nor I had the mathematical expertise to stand at the bottom of the cliff and use his measuring stick to work the problem out. So, each of us took a guess, then we split the difference, walked along the cliff until we found an easy way up it, then came back to our original line, where we might find a jack pine or two. We'd solemnly measured them — perhaps half a foot in diameter, and not a dozen feet high: occidental, hyperborean bonsai.

The summer passed. July 23rd makes a nice turning point. We had just set up camp on a new lake, a big one, five or six miles long. We were on the east side of it, on a hill, the tent nestled into a handsome spruce grove. We had learned back at Cooper Lake that a total eclipse of the sun would occur that afternoon, at about 3:30. We were given all the usual warnings about not looking directly at it, and so forth. As the time approached, we went out onto the beach to watch. We did not get the full effect. The sky darkened to the west, as though the mother of all thunderstorms were rushing towards us; the light took on a glaucous, underwater hue; the wind died. Robins and thrushes began their evening songs, then abruptly stopped, and everything was quiet. Then the cloud passed, the birds sang, the breeze resumed, and the eclipse went on, racing eastward.

People directly in the path of a total eclipse describe the apocalyptic onrush of darkness Annie Dillard describes in her great essay, "Total Eclipse." We did not experience that, but we placed ourselves in very select company by having had even a passing view of it. Its track had been incredibly narrow — 53 miles wide. It moved west to east over an almost uninhabited strip from Alaska through Canada to Maine. That same path took it over a well populated belt of Maine, including Bangor and Mt. Desert. People from away began booking accommodations in those places over a year in advance. At the time, I knew nothing about that, only that we happened to be almost beneath that speeding shadow.

In retrospect, I could, if mystically inclined, tell myself that the eclipse was directing me toward my future homeland, the way a falling star directed Aeneas on his way out of Troy. I am not mystically inclined, and, within my memory of that summer the eclipse merely marks, somewhat inexactly, the halfway point — actually, about a week past it, but late July was roughly when the atmosphere began to take on a more autumnal clarity. We still had some of those surprisingly hot days, but the shadows were growing longer and stronger, and the stars at night were about as brilliant as stars can be. In a letter home dated July 31, I described the four of us sitting in front of the tent and listening to wolves howling in the hills behind us: "Their cries drifted down to us with all the loneliness and clarity of bell music, and it seemed to be the voices of the forlorn stars themselves." *Ugh*, you will say. I cannot disagree. I was a greenhorn English major, an imposter. Anybody, including you and me, can spot it at a glance.

The next week, we had our three-day paid vacation in La Tuque, where we were put up for free at the Windsor Hotel, responsible only for our own restaurant and bar bills, which were considerable. By the time we got back to Cooper Lake and spent a few days there, we were getting cooler weather. It was beginning to feel like, as well as look like, October. The larches became beautiful, a soft tawny gold against the green of the muskegs. At

Cooper Lake, the wives of the men who ran the place, and whom we rarely saw, came up to visit. They arrived by de Haviland Beaver from Montreal; their husbands met them at the dock, and they all came trooping up the hill, speaking French, everybody elegant, vivacious, happy, and, as far as the cruisers and compass men were concerned, as exotic as a flock of parakeets or invasive tropical butterflies. Tom said this was an annual occasion at Cooper Lake, and he welcomed it. After supper one night, everybody pulled the tables and chairs in our mess hall to one side, set up a record player, and there was a dance. This was apparently an annual end-of-summer event. It was festive, singing as well as dancing. Claude was in full lounge-lizard mode. He could do the twist while standing on one leg and was much in demand. I don't think there was any drinking at all — CIP prohibited that as strictly as it prohibited open fires. We concluded by everybody going outside and singing "O Canada." In French. *Enfin!*

I think now about the responsibility that the men who oversaw the operation of the camp lived with, all summer long. Every fly that went out involved anxious consideration of the weather — dense rain or fog that could close down in a hurry, render the landscape invisible, and force Claude to find his way back to Cooper Lake by instruments alone. And even in fair weather, with that many cruisers and compass men scattered around off in the woods, there were opportunities for serious injury — a broken leg or ankle, a canoe swamped by heavy waves or heavy rapids, a fire in camp: you would not have needed a hyperactive imagination to find plenty of things to keep you awake at night. But everything had turned out happily; nobody had anything like a serious accident, or, as far as I know, even a serious head cold. The chief occupational hazard — in fact, more like an occupational certainty — was athlete's foot, brought on by putting on wet boots and socks every morning and getting them wet again the next day. The commissary always had a good supply of foot powder, and we always stocked up on it, dried our feet carefully each evening and sprinkled them liberally with anti-fungal powder the next morning. That didn't eliminate the problem but kept it under control.

A letter home from early August: "I continue to enjoy my three companions very much. I think all of us have an adequate sense of humor, and camp life offers many opportunities for it to be exercised." All true enough. Because Tom and I worked together, I knew him best, but it never occurred to me to ask him why he, a city boy from Toronto, decided to go all the way over to Frederickton and major in forestry. It might have been simple economics: he was sure of having summer jobs that paid well and let him see remote parts of Canada; it might have been that his ultimate aim, if he had one, was a desk job in Montreal. He needed coffee and a cigarette or two to become functional in the morning. He was bespectacled, bearded, funny, and, it seemed to me, smart. He wasn't exactly interested in the work we were doing, but he did it efficiently and quickly. When the four of us sat around after supper in the big dark night, he liked to play his harmonica. Nobody objected. It was miraculous, which is not to say particularly skillful, against all that emptiness — "Orange Blossom Special," "Amazing Grace," "Tennessee Waltz," but also, by request, Chubby Checker, Chuck Berry, and vintage Elvis. Then, by way of signing off, "O Canada."

During our last week of work, what had been beautiful October weather became Novemberish. Most birds left. Canada Jays did not. They became bolder and saucier, hanging around at mealtime, filching scraps. One perched on Philip's shoulder. "Looking for lice," Bob said. Out on the lake, we several times met with little flurries of snow as we paddled. The winds got stiffer; the bucket of water we kept by the stove skimmed over with ice each night. We heard wolves several more times, always at night. The Deep North was on its way to becoming the land I'd read about — the lakes frozen solid and covered with snow; the lonely travelers dogsledding or snowshoeing across them, the wind howling. Or auroras pulsing on still, long nights, and the rifle-crack of trees exploding in the cold. We left Cooper Lake at the end of August. In two weeks, I would be back in college. Then four years of graduate school and marriage, then Maine.

THE MAINE WOODS — LIVING HISTORY

If you look at a big map of Maine — not a roadmap, but a topographical map, one that shows only lakes, ponds, rivers, and streams — what you see is a transportation network that connects even the most westerly and northernly parts of the state to the sea. It was known and used for millennia before the Europeans arrived. Its great central hub is Moosehead Lake, emptying into Casco Bay via the Kennebec River. Tributaries of the Kennebec — the Dead, the Carrabassett, the Sandy, and the Androscoggin, connect it to the high country to the west, which would in time become New Hampshire and Quebec. The Moose River, which flows into the south end of Moosehead Lake, rises in Quebec, and provides another access route to the west. From the north end of Moosehead, it is a short portage to the headwaters of the West Branch of the Penobscot, which connects to the Allagash, which connects to the St. John's. The Penobscot, augmented by the East Branch, comes down to tidewater in Bangor. It and the Kennebec are the two largest rivers located entirely within Maine; the mighty St. John's of Maine and New

Brunswick is far longer and connects to the Bay of Fundy. The St. Croix, a shorter river that forms Maine's easternmost boundary with New Brunswick, is not part of the Moosehead/Penobscot/ Kennebec hub, but was connected to it by lakes, ponds, streams, and portages.

Euro-American explorers, trappers, traders, and missionaries ascended these rivers, then came loggers. The history of their endeavor is well documented within the state, and is still being written. Its early days were heroic, hazardous, and ingenious. To my knowledge, the first detailed description of it was written by John James Audubon in 1832. He spent a few September days visiting friends and collecting new species of birds in Dennysville, between Lubec and Eastport, in Down Easternmost Maine. There he and his party (which included his wife and son) were taken to see the culmination of a logging drive. Audubon's account of it constitutes one of the *Delineations of American Scenery and Character* which he interspersed throughout the *Ornithological Biography*, his description of the morphology and habits of each of the species he painted in *The Birds of America*. The *Delineations* are primarily intended for European and non-scientific readers, and especially for British ones. They celebrate the beauty and wild abundance of the American continent and incorporate descriptions of picturesque American vocations and recreations. In many of them, Audubon also celebrates himself — his adventures, his prowess afield, his encounters with famous Americans, Daniel Boon in particular. But the *Delineations* include some fine essays: e.g. his descriptions of the Ohio and Mississippi Rivers, Niagara Falls, and of a flood on the Mississippi and a powerful earthquake in Kentucky.

The essay about Dennysville is entitled "The Force of the Waters." It describes the exciting conclusion of a log drive on the Dennys River, when thousands of big logs were flushed through a narrow gorge in the lower river. Audubon prefaces this with an account of the lives of Maine "lumberers" — loggers — in the woods. His host in Dennysville, Judge Lincoln, had persuaded him to stay in town long enough to see the final stage of the drive, and had apparently told Audubon a good deal about logging. For that matter, almost anybody in town could have been a source of information. Many of the men from town worked in the log woods themselves, or in Judge Lincoln's mill, which was Dennysville's primary economic engine.

By 1833, Maine lumbermen had already become famous for their skill, hardihood, and resourcefulness. They were precisely the kind of American that the *Delineations of American Scenery and Character* intended to celebrate, ones who gave a dimension of legend to the places that Audubon's arduous pursuit of ornithological specimens had taken him.

Throughout Maine, lumbermen had to push deeper and deeper into the woods to find Bunyanesque white pines. The Dennys River, flowing out of Lake Meddybemps, is barely twenty miles long. As a short coastal river that debouched into a navigable bay, it had one important advantage: logs did not have far to travel to reach the mill, where they could be sawed and transshipped. Two important disadvantages were inseparable from its advantage: the supply of prime trees (which in this case were probably red pine and spruce, not white pine) was limited, and the river, small to begin with, became very shallow by late summer. Logs hung up and bottomed out in the shallows, particularly in the lower reaches of the river.

This problem was exacerbated by the geology of the Dennys: just before it reached tidewater and the holding pond for Judge Lincoln's mill, the river entered a narrow gorge, with vertical walls and about forty feet wide. Its bottom was obstructed with boulders and exposed ledges. Thousands of the logs coming down on the high water would form a colossal jam here, filling the gorge almost completely, and, once the spring spate was over, with only a thin trickle of water beneath them.

At the upper end of the gorge, the loggers had felled a tree tall enough to bridge it. They then propped long slabs of wood from the mill against the tree's upstream side. They fitted the slabs together tightly, so that a pond would gradually form behind them. To prop this temporary dam against the pressure of the water, they leaned long logs against its downstream side, with wooden chocks at the butt end, to hold them in place. By the time Audubon and his family were there, the dam had formed a pond ten feet deep, backing up the river for nearly a mile.

With the Audubon family, their friends, and no doubt many citizens of the town looking on, two lumberjacks walked out to the base of the dam, carrying their axes with them. Each knocked out the wedge at the bottom of the downstream prop with one blow, and then, with a second, sideways blow, knocked out the prop itself. Then they ran for their lives, jumping "with extreme dexterity from one heaving log to another" and making it back to shore "with almost the quickness of thought."

As a writer, Audubon never lapses into understatement or mere pellucidity; he fears neither the hyperextended analogy nor the cumbersome circumlocution:

> The logs bounced against each other, thrusting aside, demerging, or raising into the air those with which they came in contact....It seemed as if they were waging a war of destruction, such as ancient authors describe the efforts of the Titans, the foamings of whose wrath to the eye of the painter might have been represented by the

angry curlings of the waters, while the tremendous and rapid motions of the logs, which at times reared themselves almost perpendicularly might by the poet have been taken for the shakings of the confounded and discomfited giants.

The logs, once underway, rolled, reared, tossed and tumbled amid [sic] the foam as they were carried along....as the logs were dashed against the rocky shore, they resounded like the reports of distant artillery....It seemed to me as if I witnessed the rout of a vast army, surprised, overwhelmed, and overthrown. The roar of the cannon, the groans of the dying, the shouts of the avengers thundered through my brain.

(*Delineations of American Scenery and Character* pp. 134-136. Edited by Frances Herrick, 1926)

Phew! as Maurice might say. But Audubon's excited prose convinces at least this reader that he is very sorry to have missed that spectacle, and also to have missed its aftermath, as loggers and millhands in bateaux used steel-tipped poles and cant hooks to maneuver the logs in the mill pond into the race that fed down to Judge Lincoln's saws, converting so much forest life and forest labor into planks, beams, and cold cash.

During the 1820s, the population of Dennysville achieved its all-time high, 856 people, up from 557 the previous decade. Audubon was there early in the 1830s; by the end of the decade the population had declined by 55%, to 378. From 1850 until 1940, it was relatively stable, with an average population of about 450. Decline resumed in 1950, and by 1970, it reached its all-time low of 278. The 2020 census found the population for the second decade of the 21st century at exactly 300.

I think it's reasonable to assume that the lumbering boom reached its peak in the 1820s and that prosperity carried over into the beginning of the next decade. Given the size of the watershed, logging could not have been sustained for more than a couple of decades. The stabilization in the size of the population from the 1840s to the 1930s was probably owed to the sardine fishery. There were jobs aboard the trawlers and in the nearby canneries in Lubec and Eastport.

So, Audubon gave us a first detailed account of a logging operation in Maine. His florid description is hyperbolic, but it concisely tells the story of Maine logging. Audubon thought no harm would come from the felling of the finest trees: "Thousands of large pines . . . cut down every winter afford room for the younger trees, which spring up profusely to supply the wants of man." He was right. The trees that came up supplied the wants of man provided that what man wanted was pulpwood. A great deal of it continues to be cut in Eastern Washington County, and delivered to two big pulp mills in Baileyville, on the St. Croix River and just a few miles north of Meddybemps Lake and the headwaters of the Dennys River. One, the Woodland Mill, was built in the early 20th century; the other, the St. Croix Mill, opened in 1997 and specializes in paper for napkins, tissues, etc. It consumes 85 to 100 truckloads of wood chips every day, and operates 24 hours a day, seven days a week. The Woodland Mill is the biggest employer in Washington County, with a payroll of 310. Washington County is now the poorest county in Maine, and, all things considered, the most beautiful.

In 2017, the Natural Resources Council of Maine purchased a conservation easement on 4,707 acres along the Dennys River from International Paper Company. The primary object is preservation and enhancement of the river's annual run of Atlantic salmon, sea run trout, and herring. Traditional recreational uses — hunting, hiking, etc. — are permitted. And IP can continue wood harvest, with the proviso that the wood be harvested sustainably. The Baileyville paper mills should see no diminution of their supply of pulpwood and wood chips. This encapsulates the reality of the Unorganized Territories in Maine at this moment: an uneasy balance of preservation and a high-tech forest industry based on pulpwood monoculture.

The great book about the history of Maine logging is John S. Springer's *Forest Life and Forest Trees*, first published in 1851 by Harper Brother's of New York. It is some indication of both the ecnomic importance of the Maine woods and the appetite for stories about all facets of the logger's life that Harper Brothers put out a second edition in 1856. Thereafter, the book fell into obscurity, and had become hard to find until the New Hampshire Publishing Company reprinted it in 1971, with a helpful account of Springer's life by F. M. O'Brien of Portland.

Springer was never a stereotypical logger. Born in 1811 in Robbinston, on the St. Croix River in far eastern Washington County, he matriculated at the newly opened (1824) Maine Wesleyan Seminary, which was more than halfway across the state. His parents must have had some means, and possibly he felt a youthful attraction to the idealism of the Wesleyan movement. He seems to have remained enrolled for only a year or two before going into the woods as a logger. He worked in the woods from 1825-39, for the most part in Piscataquis County, north of Moosehead, on the mighty West Branch of the Penobscot, although he spent some time back in Washington County, in the St. Croix drainage. Logging was a complex operation in the sense that it had many specialties — teamster, timber scout, chopper, sawyer, woods boss (who decided which trees would be felled in which direction, and the route by which a team of oxen would take them to the nearest stream that was big enough to get them down to the Penobscot), swampers, who cleared the road by which teams of oxen would get the log to the river; river drivers and river bosses, who would shepherd the logs to their destination, which was usually, but not always, Bangor. He had begun logging at the age of 14 and he walked away from it fourteen years later, when he was only 28. He became an itinerant Methodist preacher, moved to Massachusetts, preached all over the state for seven years, and then retired from preaching to work on his book. It took about four years for him to complete. He obviously talked to many other loggers and former loggers: the book is full of second-hand accounts. He also assembled economic statistics regarding the quantity of wood felled and its cash value, and the comparative value of secondary species — that is, species other than white pine.

The great forests along the Penobscot and its tributaries lasted much longer than those along the Dennys, but of course they were not inexhaustible — no source of wealth on land or sea is. Lumbermen poled their bateaux farther and farther up tributary streams and roamed higher and higher into the mountains from which they flowed. Every phase of logging — locating trees, felling them, laying out roads so that, once the snow was deep enough, teams of oxen could get them down to the headwaters of a stream; then building a temporary dam to flush them downstream (and probably having to repeat this process several times, as the logs jammed again and again before reaching the West Branch, itself a tumultuous river filled with logs from ice-out to late summer — all of this grew more difficult and more dangerous every year.

His overarching motive for the book, he says, is to claim for the Maine logging industry both an economic significance and a heroic one: "a greater prominence as a source of wealth, greater respect on the ground of the talent and skill concentrated by the prime operators [i.e. the lumberjacks], greater deference for it as a business — for the endurance, energy, and courage of the thousands of hardy freemen who engage in it, and greater interest in the amount of substantial romance and adventure in the 'Life among the Loggers.'". He estimates that, on the Penobscot alone, 10,000 people were employed, in the woods, in the mills of Bangor, and in the ships that carried finished lumber — boards, beams, shingles, shakes, etc. — to ports from Maine to Florida, and to the Caribbean, the Gulf of Mexico, and Europe.

His book seems to me to succeed, and particularly in relation to the "substantial amount of romance and adventure" in life among the loggers. He was himself a skilled axman, and the describes the fierce joy of felling a huge pine, 80 feet from stump to the branching out of the crown. He speaks of such trees as the "whales of the forest," and, while he is no Melville, his book does do at least one of the things that *Moby Dick* does: it gives us a fascinating picture of an industry that is complex in its details, that typifies American hardihood, ingenuity, daring, ruthlessness, and avarice, and that is doomed by its own success.

Neil Rolde, in *The Interrupted Forest* notes that, while the adventures, dangers, and exploits of lumberjacks and river drivers did gain some fame in the latter half of the 19th century, the log woods of Maine never approached the mythic status of the Wild West. I have thought about this from time to time. The heroic era of the Maine woods, with lumberjacks, teamsters, swampers, and river bosses lasted more than two centuries; the era of the wild west, as depicted by Hollywood — cattle drives, stagecoaches, bushwhackers, gunslingers, bounty hunters, drifters, cowboy good guys and Apache or Comanche or Sioux bad guys — lasted only a few decades. The landscapes are rarely forested; action takes place against a wide horizon that hints about equally at utter emptiness and infinite possibility — no past to define or confine the solitary self; no sense of the reciprocal and cumulative consequences of history and landscapes upon each other.

In my first years of going up north for trout fishing and canoeing, logs were still being driven down the Kennebec River. When fishing there, you were always looking upstream, watching for high water. The first sign would be standing waves; the next would be the four-foot-long bolts of pulpwood among them. By the time you'd gotten ashore and had your rod taken down the river would be at full flow, with a steady stream of pulpwood going by, pitching and bobbing like a drove of sheep. Log driving on Maine Rivers was phased out in the early '70s; the very last log drive in the state took place on the Kennebec in the fall of 1976. It was high time. Sunken pulpwood and pulpwood bark littered the river and reduced its oxygen content, to the detriment of aquatic life, including trout. A spruce-budworm epidemic had devastated the woodlands throughout the unorganized territories, which led to salvage harvesting, massive clearcuts, and the establishment of a system of big logging roads, effectively antiquating rivers as a means of getting lumber to mills.

My first familiarity with Maine in general and the unorganized territories in particular led me to feel that the state's natural history and its human history managed to co-exist. The history of logging here is very old. I learned about it by reading Springer, by going to the fine Lumberman's Museum in Patten, once a major logging center on both the East Branch of the Penobscot and the Allagash, and by visiting the Maine Historical Museum in Augusta. Gradually, through that and through conversations with old timers, the Maine woods became more legible to me. Fishing on the Kennebec when the river was low, a friend picked up the rust-pocked point of a river driver's peavy, something that looks old and gruesome enough to have been welded by a Viking or an Orc. Remnants of roads run through the woods along most rivers in the unorganized townships, so overgrown that they look merely natural and geological, like eskers. But here and there you pick up the faint impressions of what were once deep ruts, worn by the cook's wagon that kept pace with the river drivers coming downstream, feeding them their four meals a day. Sometimes a single strand of wire, mounted on ceramic insulators, runs along the road — the communications technology of the Civil War adapted to the log drives.

Or you may see the rotting remnants of a sluice — a wooden aqueduct to carry logs over the jumbled terrain of a steep bank and down to the river itself — like the ones that used to be visible at the lower end of the Kennebec Gorge. A truly remarkable sluice was built by H.P. McKenney built in 1898, to get an exceptional stand of white pine lumber from Enchanted Pond down to the Dead River. The pond was drained by Enchanted Stream, so named because it runs underground in some places; in others, especially as it approaches the Dead, it passes over such a severe drop that some of McKenney's supporting trestles for the sluice were thirty feet high. The sluice took two years to build, and failure was widely predicted for it. But when at last it was completed — a mile and a quarter in all — McKenney's logs went down it with prodigious speed; he made out like a bandit. I've fished the lower end of Enchanted Stream. As far as I could see, no trace of McKenney's mighty sluice remains.

But you are always stumbling across something — an iron-framed pulpwood drag or the remnants of barns that once sheltered horses, oxen, and hay, and are now havens for chipmunks and porcupines. On the north side of the St. Johns River, down off the old road at Nine Mile Bridge there stands a self-propelled steam shovel, used in building the road that ran across the bridge. That was in 1927. The steam shovel is almost invisible in the alders and underbrush that have grown up along the old road. In one sense, it belongs in the logging museum in Patten. But the woods along Maine's major rivers are also logging museums, of the living history variety. The steam shovel in its setting looks prehistoric as well as historic — something begotten by James Watt upon a tyrannosaur. My daughter Liz and I saw it when we canoed the river twentysomething years ago. By that time, Nine Mile Bridge itself was gone, taken out by the combination of spring floods and ice floes back in the early 70s.

Not far downstream from the bridge, in an area called Seven Islands, an iron-wheeled horse-drawn hay rake stood in a big river meadow, a famous place for rare-plant specialists. It could have only been used to collect hay that had been cut down by scythes, and somewhere close by, but on higher ground, there would have been a barn for oxen or horses, teamsters to tend them and work them through the long winters, a camp with thirty or forty men felling trees, roughing out roads for the teamsters, then, after the tumult and flooding of ice-out, shepherding the logs through some tough rapids to downriver sawmills.

ADIEU

When I was in Quebec in 1963, I had no notion of futurity, not for myself, for the woods I saw, or for the Canadian International Paper Company. Legendary history is by definition a-historical. It is different from those idealizations of particular episodes of history — the Roman Republic, Periclean Athens, Elizabethan

England, Federalist America, the High Middle Ages, one *Ancien Regime* or another — that play such central roles in the politics and culture of civilizations. To the extent that I had a conscious sense of history as all, it was the product of my education, which had not at that point exposed me to Herbert Butterfield's famous definition: "History is not the study of origins; rather it is an analysis of all the mediations by which the past was turned into our present." (Herbert Butterfield, *The Whig View of History*. Legendary history would seem to be the reverse — the present invents it and gives it its approximate geographical coordinates. In the cases of the Deep North and the Wild West, although not the Deep South, its beginnings were in geology, not in some specific episode of historical time.

The mediations by which it became our present were initiated by Euro-Americans. They are more often fictional characters than historical ones.

My own present is that of an old man. For me, as for many Euro-Americans, the sense of history has turned out to be rooted in geography. Literally rooted, in many cases — woods and forests, but also in individual trees: the uses we make of them and the news they give us about the planet. This began even before I had that wonderful summer in Northern Quebec, working for CIP.

In 1931, when Butterfield wrote, the idea of environmental history as either a cause or an effect of human history had scarcely been articulated. Rachel Carson's *Silent Spring*, published the year before my summer in Quebec, marked a turning point. The first Earth Day was celebrated in 1970. James Hansen's *Storms of My Grandchildren* takes it as a given that a tipping point has been passed. He is one year older than I am; our grandchildren will share the same fate. Even if the reductions in carbon dioxide emissions called for by the Paris Accords of 2018 are achieved, our grandchildren will live in what amounts to a new geological era: fire, flood, rising sea levels, intolerable extremes of temperature, inevitable cascades of extinction: cf. Elizabeth Kolbert's *The Sixth Extinction*.

I have never returned to the country north of La Tuque. At first, I was so busy in the thick and fast of my own life — graduate school, marriage, teaching, children, living in Maine and coming to know it — that I felt no impulse to go back up there. I had all the Deep North I could absorb all around me. Gradually, as over decades I saw the changes in logging practices that have happened here, I lost any desire to go back. The barracks at the log camps would no longer house *bucherons*. The chain saw would have been replaced by the feller-buncher and the whole tree chipper; the roads would have been improved, and huge tractor-trailer trucks loaded with logs or wood chips, would roar down them, carrying those beautiful, mossy spruce-fir forests to the mills of La Tuque and Three Rivers.

Spring is always the season when the danger of forest fires is at its greatest in the Deep North. That was true in 1963, when my arrival at Cooper Lake was postponed for two weeks because all the cruisers and compass men were fighting fires up around James Bay. But when they broke out this spring — 2023 — they proved uncontainable. The weather had gotten too warm too soon, the snow had melted too early, the summer rains never came. Canada's Deep North and the provinces that comprise it are so vast that Americans (and most Canadians, for that matter) have a hard time comprehending it. Two weeks ago, we were told that an area twice the size of New Jersey had been destroyed. Last week, the fire had grown into an area somewhat larger than South Carolina. That is easy for me to imagine in that I'm familiar with South Carolina's distances, many of its rivers, and some of its great variety of habitats. It is impossible for me to conceive of it all ablaze or already blackened.

And so, for me, Cooper Lake and all those nameless lakes, rivers, bogs, and streams surrounding it have become an autobiographical version of legendary geography. And CIP, as I experienced it in 1963, now belongs to a different age in the history of logging. It has been a great pleasure and a great self-indulgence for me to try to recall as much of that natural ecosystem and that human one as accurately as I can.

So far, Maine has had none of the smoke from the Canadian fires that in early June made the sun rising over the Manhattan skyline look like a brilliantly orange harvest moon, and the city like sepia-tinted ghost town. As of early July, our summer has been unusually cool and damp. We've escaped the floods, fires, and record-shattering heat the rest of the country has had. Friends in Oregon, Montana, Chicago, New Orleans, and South Carolina tell us about it. We are tempted to think that by next year or the year after, those places, our hemisphere, our globe, and our grandchildren's future will be restored. It is an illusion without a future.

A Voice Crying in the Wilderness

This essay was written for the anthology Wolf, *privately printed in 2012, in an effort to overturn Michigan's recent decision to legalize wolf hunting in the state. That effort was successful. Wolf hunting has, however, been legalized in other states: e.g. Idaho, Montana. And, of course, in Alaska, where for many years shooting them from slow, low-flying, airplanes was a legal and popular way for wealthy alpha couch potatoes to collect trophies for themselves. Since 2014, however, they have had to hire guides and hunt on foot.*

L et me first establish that I am a hunter and have been for seventy years. So, I start with feelings of friendly respect for any alpha predator.

I live in Maine, not yet a battleground state in the wolf wars. But there's still hope. Fifty-five years ago, critters started showing up in our north woods, and people at first thought they were wolves, or wolf-dogs; then they thought coy-dogs — dog-coyote hybrids. Turned out they were eastern brush coyotes; analysis of their DNA implicated both the gray wolf and the domestic dog in their ancestry. In any event, they were big enough to raise the usual ruckus: they would decimate the deer herd, slaughter sheep, raid henhouses, cathouses, cradles. No such luck. They've now spread into just about every nook and eco-cranny in the east, all the way down to Florida. And they have proven totally inadequate to controlling our major pest species, the white-tailed deer.

I get it that wolf-coyote hybrids are not the same thing as the gray wolf, aka timber wolf. Wolves are powerful and relentless; a pack of them is the closest thing this country has had to a well-regulated militia since the Revolution. They are strikingly intelligent, and look so much like the finest, truest, most perfect dog ever to grace this planet that you want to make friends with them. Don't bother; they have already succeeded in being what they are meant to be, and they know it.

We settled this country by shooting first and asking questions later: red wolves, grey wolves, timber wolves, wolverines, bears, cougars, coyotes, Native Americans: whatever frightened us. This kind of behavior is habit-forming, so now we shoot each other, wholesale, and fill our gun closets with weapons suited for no other purpose. But we cannot pretend that we're frontiersmen, competing with other alpha predators for a limited protein supply. More and more of us live out our lives in cities and suburbs and cyberspace.

But a lot of us go outdoors, hunting or hiking or skiing or sledding or surfing. It's healthy and soul-soothing and so forth, but face it: we also go there in order to experience a trace of fear, awe, loneliness, exhilaration, the chance of going on and on, losing ourselves — each of those possibilities dependent on the others; all of them amounting to a sort of shiver down the spine. Even if we don't actually do these things, we like to imagine that we do, and watch movies and television shows about them. An old poet, recalling being out alone at night, up to some minor mischief, spoke of the "ministry of fear." A need for it is hardwired into us.

A Voice Crying in the Wilderness

Sixty years ago this year, I spent the summer as an understudy to a timber cruiser in northern Quebec. We cruised roadless country that had never been cut. A float plane flew us over miles and miles of spruce, fir, birch, larch jack pine, lakes, muskeg, granite; set us down in the middle of somewhere with a canoe, food, a tent, and a map showing us specific spots where we were to go to count and measure trees. My cruiser and I usually traveled with another cruiser and his assistant, staying a week or so in one place, then being picked up, resupplied, and put down in the middle of somewhere else. It was a paid adventure, with just enough responsibility and discomfort to make us feel important, and we enjoyed it.

In June the twilight had gone on and on, barely dying out to the west before the its first adumbrations began in the east. But by August the dark came earlier and quicker. We'd sit around the fire and talk after supper. The loons that had been part of the long evenings no longer had much to say. One of the cruisers had a harmonica, and he might squeak away at that for a while. The fire and the music, such as it was, made the night and the woods and the big lakes all that much bigger, a mighty surrounding silence and invisibility. The four of us were barely out of adolescence, old enough to draft but not to vote, full of the big talk and bravado that come from knowing, deep down inside yourself, that you don't know shit.

One night, past midnight, I went out to piss. The moon was down, the sky was utterly black and the stars, numberless as the sands of the sea or the sins of the forefathers, glittered starkly. Frost was in the air and the night was so still that you could hear yourself breathing.

203

First there was a yip that tried to prolong itself, and then another; then a howl that rose, full-throated and full of power, wavering and quavering on and on. This from our side of the lake, and probably not close, although it was so startling that it seemed close. Then from across the lake an answer, the sound carrying over the water and spreading echoes in its wake. It *was* close. The howling, some of it shrill and puppyish, became general, call and response from one shore of the lake to the other. It sounded more forlorn than frightening, and it seemed, from where I stood, directed upward and outward, as though the wolves felt a mighty craving for something infinite and intangible.

Years of explaining everything that happens have passed, and I can tell myself that what I felt in Quebec was that my life had at last become like something out of a book, and that is because wolves — gray, indistinct, just beyond the circle of flickering light where the lost child sits shivering — lurk around the shadows of so many children's stories, symbolizing the fears we secretly love. But at the time I felt that hearing those wolves *meant* something. It had to. It was a variety of religious experience, in the same way that falling in love is: it does not commit you to a creed; it does commit you to trying to be worthy of something you in no way deserved or ever truly expected.

As a country, we rely on the bottom line to settle every argument. Or so we say. But we also, collectively and individually, disregard it, and live beyond our means. Wolf hunts won't generate much revenue; wolf predation won't have a measurable impact upon Michigan's GDP. We aren't going to settle this matter by arithmetic and bookkeeping. Wolves have haunted the psyche of Eurasia and North America out of all proportion to the dangers they pose. The reason for that is because they are so beautiful, so much like the dogs we have domesticated and yet so superior to them. We ourselves seem a bit small and shabby by comparison. For some people, that is exactly why we should kill them; for the rest of us, that is exactly why we should not.

What Else Remains?

This essay was written for Voices from the Coast, *a collection of poems, essays, photographs, and paintings celebrating the 50th anniversary of Maine Coast Heritage Trust in 2020. MCHT serves as an umbrella organization for the many local land trusts devoted to preservation of land, habitats, and viewsheds along the Maine coastline and its offshore islands.*

Once the head of tide on the Kennebec River was up around Bingham. Along what we think of as the Maine coast, from Kittery to Calais, the deep and dark blue ocean rolled. The great whales and great auks fed and frolicked; gannets plummeted, porpoises tumbled. No human eye saw them. Longfellow's "beautiful town/ That is seated by the sea," lay far below and far ahead of them.

Europeans arrived; human and natural history began their incessantly escalating struggle. Human history wins most of the battles, thereby accelerating its eventual loss of the war. Think of Boston's Back Bay — Commonwealth Avenue, Beacon, Boylston, and Newberry Streets, the Boston Public Library, the Prudential Center: some of the priciest urban real estate north of Manhattan. It was tidewater a mere two centuries ago. Where commuters now creep along Storrow Drive, the Abenaki built fish weirs. Think of Portland's Back Cove: in Longfellow's Day, Marginal Way, lower Preeble Street, outer Franklin Avenue, and a long stretch of I-295 lay within the jurisdiction of the Harbor Master, as did Baxter Boulevard.

Well south of New England, along most of the alluvial shoreline that from Sandy Hook, New Jersey, down to Florida, coastal development came belatedly but suddenly, to places that had beaches, and for people who had leisure. Within living memory — mine — lonely beaches and barrier islands became sleazy or upscale tourist meccas, retirement destinations, or swanky gated communities, complete with world-class golf courses.

In low-lying country, a little sea rise goes a long way. Ask citizens of Atlantic City, Norfolk and Virginia Beach, Wilmington, Charleston, or Miami about sunny day floods and king tides. People are clever and resourceful — Holland is proof of that — and these cities may well survive for quite some time, surrounded by dykes and drained by pumps. But imagine yourself flying the 500 or so miles from Sandy Hook, New Jersey down to the bottom of North Carolina. You'd mostly see variations of one pattern: barrier islands facing the open Atlantic, and between them and the mainland, interconnected bays and sounds — Barnegat, Rehoboth, Assawoman, Sinepuxent, Chincoteague, Currituck, Albemarle, Pamlico. The barrier islands are basically sandspits. Some remain beautifully empty. Many are anything but: Atlantic City, Ocean City, or Avalon, New Jersey; Rehoboth Beach, Delaware; Ocean City, Maryland; Chincoteague and Virginia Beach, Virginia. In North Carolina, Nag's Head, Kitty Hawk, Corolla, Surf City, Topsail Island, and Wrightsville Beach. You see narrow strips of houses and hotels perched on sand a few feet above sea level, cut off from higher and dryer land by open water or inland swamp. The scientific consensus is that no amount of beach replenishment or fortification can save them; the data is indisputable, but not undeniable. In 2011, the political leadership of North Carolina passed HB 819, ruling the scientific consensus out of order, null and void, whenever it threatened to undermine property values.

I've never flown over the coast I've just described. But I know it by analogy to the South Carolina coast. I was lucky to grow up there. And I cannot bear going back to the beaches and inlets I knew. I can see them in my sleep, but only there.

But I have flown up the Maine Coast, from Portland to Lubec, in a private plane that Bowdoin college chartered to take a few faculty to Grand Manan. We left early, on serene June morning. We followed the coastline the whole way out to Lubec, before we turned east across the Grand Manan channel. We maintained an altitude of perhaps a thousand feet.

I know particular parts of the Maine Coast intimately; so does everybody who is reading this. We can see them in our sleep. But dear God, think of the whole length of it! That string of bays, sounds, and tidal rivers; rockbound peninsulas, spruce-crowned ledges, and gently rolling salt-water farms; the orderly scatter of islands. Think of the salt-marshes, the sequestered and unspoiled little beaches: all that Real Estate.

This coast fosters some kind of belief in permanence. Artists have made it part of our national heritage: think of Fitzhugh Lane, Frederic Edwin Church, Winslow Homer, Rockwell Kent, John Marin, the Wyeths, Eliot Porter, and so many, many others. Or think of a single poem — Elizabeth Bishop's "North Haven." Or one book, Rachel Carson's *The Edge of the Sea.*

In human history, economic history, and natural history, everything connects to everything else and nothing is permanent. Southward from Sandy Hook, New Jersey, and N.C. HB 819 notwithstanding, billions of dollars of investment and a lot of good memories will soon be lost: hotels and houses and skinny beachfront towns, built on sand and surrounded by water, will disappear in another fifty years. Investment writes off its losses, leaves its failures to be dealt with people who cannot themselves leave, and moves on. Life covets coastlines, and no species is more covetous than ours. All that investment and all those people who want to live by the ocean will soon be going elsewhere, and where would that be? Northeastward from Portland. On this coast of America, what else remains?

The great American heritage of landscape painting began with the Hudson River School. The paintings still exist; the Hudson River that the painters saw with their eyes and felt in their bones does not. This is not the case in Maine. We can see what the painters saw, miles and miles of it, recognize it, and still feel it in our bones. That is a rare and remarkable thing.

Any heritage, artistic or natural, is an endowment or a trust, and requires funding. The aim is simple: continuity and perpetuation. MCHT turns fifty this year. It has continued and coordinated the efforts of many land trusts and many individuals — some local, and some from Away — to carry into the unforeseeable, uncontrollable future a heritage that is national, regional, and local; historical, ecological, cultural, and alive.

Autobondage

*In April 2002, the Maine Olmsted Alliance hosted a conference on
cultural landscapes and roadway design in Maine. Called "Beyond
the Pavement," the conference explored how design standards used in
roadway projects enhance or diminish the visual quality of landscapes
and communities. One of the organizers of the conference was an old
friend, and asked me to give an introductory talk.*

*I knew nothing about the topic, but had longstanding admiration
for Olmsted, both as a landscape architect and as the author of* The
Cotton Kingdom, *an 1861 collection of articles he wrote about the
South.*

*My talk was subsequently published in the Olmsted Alliance
newsletter.*

I have taught mostly medieval English at Bowdoin College
for thirty-something years. That is the extent of my qualification to give this talk. As I was beginning to work on it, I
happened to hear on public radio that this year marks the 100th
anniversary of the founding of the American Automobile Association. That is the extent of my research on the topic of this talk.
Given the laughably insubstantial nature of my qualifications
and preparations, it is perhaps appropriate that the talk turns out
to be something between a ghost story and an April Fool's joke.

In honor of the founding of the American Automobile Association, I will ask you to imagine a spring evening — April 1st to be exact — in 1902. A middle-aged, small, and strikingly brisk woman takes her evening walk. She is going down a lane through an orchard on a low ridge, on the western outskirts of Lexington, Massachusetts. She pauses to admire the way the last of the sunlight falls on the ridge across the valley from her. A hundred years later, where she pauses will be in the middle of the median strip of I-95.

The woman's given name is Abigail. But as a child she loved the trains that ran through Lexington, and her childish mispronunciation of *choo choo* earned her the nickname of Choochee. Her elderly relations said it sounded like the name of some wild Indian savage out of a novel by Mr. Cooper. But it stuck. Grave and saintly Mr. Emerson, of Concord, told her it was a fine name, exactly the sort of name an American should have. Americans should always invent their own names, he said: new bottles for new wine.

So, Choochee it remains. She is still fond of trains, of movement and of travel. Charlie, her favorite nephew, owns an automobile, and takes her riding in it. It is even better than the train. She relishes the hullabaloo their passing creates among the roadside horses, dogs, chickens, and children, and among her elderly relations, peering from behind their curtains and saying, "Merciful heavens. Is that *Abigail* in that contraption?"

And there is also something more important to like about it. The rush of air against her face makes her feel less earthbound. In early childhood, she had once walked with her parents along the Boston waterfront. She had looked up at the figureheads thrusting out beneath the bowsprits of the clippers that were docked there. One of them stood for all of them. It was a woman, staring wide-eyed ahead of her. Her mane of red hair and her midnight blue robes swept back and lapped over the bow of the ship. For years Choochee imagined that figure at sea, straining and plunging toward a limitless, unattainable horizon. It filled her with longing. It was gratifying, amid the circumscribed realities of middle age, to feel the air against her face and the reinvigoration of that longing. It reminded her that she had a soul, anachronistic though such a notion had begun to seem.

She also likes Charlie's sporty insouciance when he gets behind the wheel, pulls on his gauntlets, and adjusts his goggles. She picks up his breezy way of talking; they refer to his vehicle as an auto. Her husband objects — Next thing you'll be calling a locomotive a loco, he says. But she is undeterred. Auto is right. A pure prefix, unencumbered by a noun. Nouns are persons, places, or things. An auto is not exactly any of those things, or perhaps a bit of all of them. So auto it will be. New bottles for new wine, she tells her husband, settling the matter.

Now she stands in the orchard looking northeastward, over the wide, shallow valley with its marshy stream winding down the middle, and toward the ridge opposite hers. Its crest still glows in the evening light. The slopes and valley are quilted with fields, hedgerows, pastures, stone fences, and orchards, and gerrymandered by roads and lanes. Down in the shadows, from the marshes along the stream, she hears the distant cacophony of blackbirds and grackles, their metallic voices rising into the coming darkness, like a ragged orchestration of unoiled ratchets and pulleys.

You form this vision of her a hundred years later — April 1, 2002 — as you sit in the northbound traffic west of Boston on I-95, looking across the shallow valley towards the opposite ridge, a mile away. Ahead of you, four lanes of ruby-red taillights flare, stop, and stutter across the valley and up to the crest of the opposite hill. On the other side of the median, four lanes of headlights crawl down the ridge and across the valley toward you. An occasional tractor trailer inches along, looming up above the sedans and SUVs like a battleship in the middle of a fleet of pleasure boats.

Then you imagine yourself translated from your landscape to hers, materializing beside her in the dusk as she stands in the orchard. The same magic that brings you there allows you to project I-95, with its rush hour traffic, its overpasses and contoured exit ramps and big office complexes and development parks upon the landscape she has been regarding.

She stares at this apparition. You explain it to her. You point out the few topographical features of her world that will still be ascertainable a century later-the dips and lifts of the ridgeline on the other side of the valley, the brushy ditch that preserves the general course of the stream where the grackles and blackbirds were calling. Nothing remains of the quilted fields and the hedgerows, the barns and garden plots and farmhouses. Nothing remains of the livestock whose whinnying, blearing, mooing, crowing, squealing, and braying were the white noise, the Muzak of everyday life.

In its scale and its effect on the landscape, the monstrous roadway in front of her might as well be a glacier. The mass of cars and trucks on it is ominously silent, without the banging, rattling, and clattering that she associates with motorized transport. She momentarily has the impression that the road, with its sleek black surface, is a giant conveyor belt. The individual vehicles are sinister, especially the oncoming ones with their bright glowing eyes and orthodontic grillwork. Their glossy carapaces suggest some new order of exoskeletal invertebrates-gigantic trilobites or centipedes.

But Choochee is not some quaint, sweetly befuddled incarnation of our sentimental or condescending pieties about the past.

As a young woman of quietly independent mind, she had attended the lectures of Professor William James, of Harvard College, and had considered them deeply. She concluded that his views on religion were as accurate as it was possible for views on religion to be, and had felt freed, rather than devastated, by the conclusion. Her mother's second cousin, Oliver Wendell Holmes, had just been chosen for the Supreme Court. Choochee had no doubt that he would do brilliantly there. She thought he argued better than any man alive, but she also privately believed that the law and its minions were more bottle than wine. She preserved her mother's habit of referring to Cousin Oliver as the Young Bore, to distinguish him from his famous father.

Mr. Emerson of Concord, who had approved of her nickname, was the one great spirit she had known. She never asserts this or seeks to prove it; she simply knows it in her heart. He was already drifting into senility as she was emerging into young womanhood, and his books began drifting into mere inert respectability not long after that. But even when he was very old, his fine face still looked outward and onward, and the recollection of it is as emblematic to her as the figurehead on the clipper ship. He is the true sponsor, patron, and friend of the inner life, its freedom and primacy over all things. Her single guiding conviction comes from him: that the divine order, the natural order, the social order, the economic order-all must be consecrated to the individual, and not the other way around. The many paradoxes and lapses and leaps of logic in his books do not trouble her. She reads him as some people read their bibles, not seeking for a systematic doctrine bur for paragraphs, aphorisms, phrases, and images that leap from his world to hers, with the force of oracles or revelations.

She now begins to ask you questions. At first, she assumes that what you have shown to her is some stupendous event in her country's future — an exodus, a migration, a mobilization, or a grand exposition like the one in Chicago.

No, you explain to her. No. This is a daily occurrence. It happens outside the old eastern cities like Boston and New York and Philadelphia, and outside the newer midwestern ones like Chicago and Cleveland. But it also happens in and around places that she knows of only as villages, if she knows of them at all: Houston, Wichita, Denver, Los Angeles, Seattle. Toronto, Calgary, Vancouver. Nairobi, Lagos, Sao Paolo, Buenos Aires, Sidney. And around the ancient, legendary cities of her civilization — Jerusalem, Athens, Rome, Paris, London. Twice a day the stream of traffic thickens and slows; the massed vehicles press and nudge forward, each vehicle curbing within itself the power of scores and hundreds of horses. Twice a day, the pent energy pulses and vibrates in the air. The sun never sets on it.

—How did it happen? She asks. When?

And so, deploying the magic at your disposal, you show her. Beginning with a car like her nephew's, and trading it every five years or so, you travel outward and onward from Lexington and from 1902. You crisscross the continent; you travel through wars, booms, depressions, eras of national crisis and national complacency. Every second or third day, you enter a new decade.

As early as 1909, you learn from the *Scientific American* that "the automobile has practically reached the limit of its development." And you quickly learn that that was like saying that an acorn had practically reached the limit of its development. Wars accelerated aeronautical development, and aeronautical and automotive development fed off each other. You could see that the long-nosed V-8 Ford roadsters preferred by John Dillinger and

Clyde Barrow in the 1930s co-evolved with the Spitfires and Messerschmitts that fought over the green fields of England a decade later. You could see it again in the aerodynamic contours of the Saber jet and the tail-finned, two-toned Plymouth Fury hardtop that you drove through the late 50s. Always the cars became faster and smoother; to accommodate all that speed, the roads became wider and better engineeered. To take advantage of the improved roads, the cars became yet more powerful, requiring the roads to become yet bigger, and so forth.

So, you and she drive, faster and faster every decade. Days, miles, and years blur inro each other. A few scenes, a few events are frozen in their frames, and stick in memory. In one, the two of you stand beside the car beside a river. Spanish moss sways in a cypress above your heads, the odor of jessamine surrounds you, and a ferry, running on an overhead cable like a trolley car, angles across the river toward you, to carry you over. In another, you are parked in front of a hardware store in a dusty west Texas town. A man wheels out a steel drum on a handcart, sets it up on the boardwalk, unscrews the threaded bung, and uses a hand pump with a tube attached to fill the car with gas, and to top off the two supplemental tanks that are bolted to the running board. And then it is a sunny weekday morning, and you are, astonishingly, the only automobile in sight on the world's first complex of urban expressways, overpasses, and cloverleafs. This is Los Angeles, California, the self-proclaimed city of the future, but it is 1943, a war is on, fuel is rationed, and the future, for the moment, seems in doubt.

But then after the war, fueled by the war, the pace picks up. The cars now have seats like sofas; they have radios and tinted windows. In their design and in the way they are advertised, it is all but explicit — they have replaced haystacks, barns, and cheap hotels as the preferred sites for illicit assignation. Suburbs and subdivisions and bedroom communities arise; a new kind of American neighborhood begets a new kind of American sociology, and even a new kind of American. Towns and cities sprawl and merge; beltways and connectors and central arteries link communities and kill neighborhoods, and always the pace accelerates, the construction projects growing larger and larger. Chief among their unintended consequences will be the need for yet more and yet larger projects.

You seem to encounter an outcome of these developments on a summer day in 1995. Driving through Utah, you find yourselves in the middle of a loose caravan of RVs. One passes you on a descending grade, you pass it on the next ascending grade, and this game goes on for the rest of the afternoon. Each time you pass, the man at the wheel cuts his eyes briefly in your direction, then stares stonily ahead. He wears sunglasses, and his white baseball cap proclaims *You're as Young as You Feel.* Each time you are passed, you get the profile of his wife. She does not glance your way at all. Her eyes are also fixed forward, and she has the remote, unblinking, unseeing look of a soldier braced at attention, or of the Statue of Liberty. Choochee looks at her, recalls that figurehead on the clipper ship, and says something under her breath.

On the side of the RV is painted, in glowingly soft and mellow pastels, a scene of snowcapped mountains, with a bald eagle flying across the foreground, and underneath, a caption in gothic script, *America the Beautiful.* Next to the AARP sticker on the rear bumper another sticker announces *We're spending our kids' inheritance.*

You ask Choochee to repeat her remark. *New bottles for old vinegar*, she says, with an asperity that has grown sharper over the last few decades.

Finally, it is the evening of April 1, 2002, and the two of you are stuck in the rush-hour traffic on I-95, on the ridge where the orchard was, looking across the valley where the blackbirds sang their wheezy songs. For a long time now — for days, for decades — you have not felt that you were moving through real time and real space. Your current vehicle has a CD player, a television screen that folds down from the ceiling, an on-board navigational system, a cellular telephone. The analogy now is not to a military aircraft but to a station in outer space. The big interstates become their own medium, with their own scenery, their own commerce and culture. They in effect constitute a new region of the country, densely populated, and exceptionally well represented in Congress. They offer nothing for memory to attach itself to or for curiosity to investigate, nothing to make you linger. Time is distance; distance is time, and all the other dimensions of travel have disappeared.

Choochee has to be getting back now. She has some things to do before the fall of 1918, when the Red Sox will win the pennant, and before that winter, when she will lie down and die, a victim of the great influenza epidemic. But before you part the two of you will do one more thing. You will do what people, and especially people from Massachusetts, generally do when they feel claustrophobic, overwhelmed, and stressed out. You will drive up to Maine for a few days.

And so you do — cross over at Kittery, go up the turnpike, then 95, then Route 1, then turn back inland at Wiscasset, cross over the pretty little river at the cluster of fine old Colonial houses at Sheepscot village, then up the west side of Damariscotta Lake to Jefferson, then eastward, then north through Washington and Liberty, staying west of Hope, which is not on your itinerary. The afternoon is fading as you approach the little town of Freedom, which stands well to the southeast of Unity, but considerably northwestward of Union.

Since you left Route 1, it seems as though you have been driving in reverse, over roads that are heaved by frost and follow the contours of the earth. You feel closer to the middle of the 20th century than to the beginning of the 21st. A few dairy farms remain; there are many low boggy pastures filling in with alders, pines edging out into fields, mucky little stock ponds choked with cattails and bullrush, beaver flowages full of dead standing trees. Everything is pleasingly disheveled; the passage of time is still registered by vegetative succession, by woods reclaiming orchards, by deer drifting out of them at dusk, to graze where once a fine herd of guernseys had. Outside Freedom you take a road that runs along a ridge, and stop there to look out over the upper Sheepscot valley. You talk a while; from below, you hear the metallic racket of blackbirds and grackles.

Then you explain to her about the Maine Olmsted Alliance for Parks and Landscapes — how tomorrow morning you are supposed to say something about highways, landscapes, and history. You have shown her pretty much everything you know on the subject. What should you say?

Well, that's easy, she says. Highways bury landscapes; they erase history. That is their nature. There is comparatively little the Maine Olmsted Alliance can do about it.

Is it so bleak as all that? you ask. Can't we at least mitigate, limit the damage, save the villages and towns, preserve the rural character?

From what I have seen, she says, That will solve no problems. It will simply relocate them.

You sit for a while. Then she says

I will not be here much longer. You will not see me again. Listen.

Mr. Emerson believed in Liberty, Freedom, Union, Unity
— all of that. Here is something he said. He said a man need
only get in a carriage or go up in a balloon to suddenly see his
town as nothing more than a puppet show. Everything seems to
become unreal. Or, as he might put it now, all reality becomes
virtual reality — what is seen through the windshield becomes
merely an image, like the one on the video screen. We feel no
connection, responsibility, or affection for it, except as it may di-
vert or displease us as we pass through.

Mr. Emerson thought travel wonderful in this way. It de-
tached you from your physical circumstances and showed them
to be mere illusions; it showed you that what was finally and truly
real was your own mind. That and only that.

When Charlie would take me to ride in his auto, the dogs
and the people of Lexington would suddenly look to us like characters on a stage, put there for our amusement. I often thought
of Mr. Emerson. I knew he would approve of the auto. Auto
means self you know — the self as Mr. Emerson understood it,
free, individual, autonomous, and autotelic. I imagined that
someday, without buying any tickets or consulting any schedules,
every single American woman and man would be able to step
into an auto, free themselves from pedestrian circumstances, and
know they had souls. Internal combustion: I loved the idea of
that. We are not puppets twitched by strings or dray carts pulled
by horses, I thought. We propel ourselves by an inward burning.

And now I have seen what you have shown me, the fulfill-
ment of my wish. It is bitter. Roadways have replaced our circumstances. They disenchant our restlessness. They destroy their
destinations. We can think of no way to escape them except by
extending them. New Hampshire's motto is out of date. It should
now read, *Drive or Be Driven*.

And I fear Mr. Emerson may also require revision. He wrote

that all history was biography. He meant all American history, that we would make it by our individual lives. "But all American history in the century you have shown me is autobiography."

Things are now growing gauzy and insubstantial in the fading light.

I must go back now, she says.

Should we all try to do that, you ask.

What?

Go back. Try to return to that lane through the apple orchard outside Lexington. You gesture toward the valley, where the scattered lights of the houses are coming on, and a few cars travel homeward. "What is here does not seem impossibly far from it."

She smiles, her teeth very white in the gloom. No, no. You must go through with it. The past is a dream. It will mean only what you choose to make of it, and you will never understand it in the normal way you understand your own life.

And so, a century from now, where we sit now will be a median strip, and eight solid lanes of headlights and taillights will stretch across this valley?

I cannot tell you that. I can tell you that a century from now the American Automobile Association will be a quaint anachronism. A century from now on this ridge or the one in Lexington, your ghost will be as amazed by what it sees as mine was, four days and a century ago. But I cannot at all tell you what it will see.

Now she is barely visible. In some pool or bog nearby, wood frogs are beginning.

Think of those names, her voice says out of the darkness.

Names?

Yes. Washington, Jefferson, Liberty, Unity, Freedom, even Hope. They were named that so that people would not forget that it is possible to break away from their past, not so that they would wish to return to it.

But can we? Here in Maine? In these little towns?

It will not be easy, her voice replies. But yes. It happened before.
In little towns, villages really.

Little towns like?

Yes, she says, and you see her teeth shine briefly. It is impossible
to tell if the smile is rueful or radiant. "*Little towns like Concord,*
like Lexington, Massachusetts. Liberty, Freedom, and Hope began
there. Remember that.

Then it was dark, and she was gone, and I am through.

FRANKLIN BURROUGHS is the Harrison King McCann Research Professor of the English Language Emeritusat Bowdoin
College, where he taught English literature from1968 to 2002.
His essays have appeared in a vaiety of literary publications and
anthologies, including *Best American Essays, The Pushcart Anthology,* and *The Norton Anthology of Nature Writing.* A recipient of
a National Endowment of the Arts fellowship, he is the author
of the books *The River Home, Billy Watson's Croker Sack,* and
Confluence. He lives in Topsham, Maine.